THE TRUTH ABOUT
WORLD FINANCIAL GROUP
UNAUTHORIZED

Steve Siebold

DOWNLOAD THE WORKBOOK
www.WFGWORKBOOK.com

The Truth About World Financial Group

Steve Siebold

Published by
London House
www.londonhousepress.com

ISBN: 978-0-9965169-4-5

TABLE OF CONTENTS

WATCH

WORLD FINANCIAL GROUP

VIDEO DOCUMENTARY

WWW.WFGMOVIE.COM

STUDY

FULL INTERVIEWS OF WFG STARS

WWW.WFGSTARS.COM

PURCHASE

ADDITIONAL COPIES OF THE BOOK

WWW.WFGBOOK.COM

INTRODUCTION

In 1984, I was a broke college student who wanted to be rich. I was attending the University of South Alabama in Mobile, and I wasn't all that enthused about what I was learning in my business classes. The professors warned us of the risks of starting a business and encouraged their students to seek employment with a large corporation that offered competitive salaries, benefits and long-term job security.

While their intentions were good, their advice didn't resonate with me. All the talk about safety and security wasn't turning me on, and I grew increasingly frustrated. Of all the rich people I knew from my days as a competitive junior tennis player, I couldn't recall a single one who didn't have his or her own business. And playing it safe wasn't their style.

On February 10, 1984, I was approached by a man in a parking lot near the university who asked me if I was interested in making extra money. I said yes, and he invited me to a meeting that evening about a mile from my dorm. I arrived at seven p.m., and there were 10 people jammed into a small apartment. The presenter showed up a few minutes later in a three-piece suit, carrying a white board. He was introduced as an engineer with Internation- al Paper Company in Mobile.

For over an hour, he talked about money, dreams and starting your own business. He talked about how investing 40 years of your life with a big company was outdated and how he had found a better way. At the end of his presentation, he said the opportunity he represented was Amway.

I had never heard of Amway, but I was excited. The man gave us an oversized yellow envelope with a cassette tape inside and told us to take it home and listen to it. The tape I listened to was by a man named Kay Fletcher. He talked about what it was like going from being broke to being rich and that he had done it through Amway.

I listened to the hour-long tape three times that night. The message was what I had expected to hear in my college classes but never did. It was the greatest recording I had ever heard. I felt like a starving soul that had just been fed, and somehow I knew my life would never be the same. It wasn't. I joined Amway soon after and sold toothpaste and laundry detergent out of my dorm. I recruited 13 other students to join me and earned overrides on their sales. I attended meetings, conventions and sales rallies across the southeast, and I enjoyed them.

I learned more from being in Amway than I did in college. Every business I built from that point forward was shaped by what I learned in Amway. I never earned any substantial money in Amway, but the millions I've earned since can all be traced back to that experience.

In 2005, my first book, 177 Mental Toughness Secrets of the World Class, became a best seller. The book was selling to sales organizations by the case, and one of those organizations was World Financial Group.

In 2006, the company invited me to address their leadership team in Las Vegas, which was comprised of about 500 top performers. Since then I've spoken at WFG meetings, conventions and seminars to over 100,000 WFG associates. I've worked one-on-one with many of the highest-ranking associates and gotten to know them on a personal level. I've listened to their stories at my book signings, and through phone, email and personal letters over the past 13 years. I can say with some measure of authority that I know these people. I know how they think and what makes them tick.

Just to be clear, I am not nor ever have been, associated with World Financial Group in any way, outside of being a vendor. They did not pay me to write this book, nor did they have any editorial control over its content. The purpose of an unauthorized work is having the freedom to explore aspects of the opportunity that no corporate compliance department would allow in an authorized version. It's easy to find the upside and benefits of WFG by visiting their website or reading their promotional pamphlets.

But if you're going to devote your time and energy to a controversial method of making money, you want to know the good, bad and ugly upfront.

My promise, dear reader, is to take you behind the scenes and give you a three-dimensional view of this explosive opportunity and the stars that drive it.

The content you're about to consume is based on:

13-years of behind the scenes observation

107-interviews with field leaders, failed associates, employees, former employees, product providers, competitors, and MLM critics and experts; and

6-months and over 1,200 hours of writing and research with a five-person staff.

This book presents the truth about WFG, or at least as I've experienced and researched it, so you can make a decision as to whether or not to get involved. It should be used only as a guide, as one piece of your investigative, due diligence process.

My goal is to inform, not to persuade. After years of reading criticism of this company on the Internet, I thought it was time for an objective outsider, with an inside track and nothing to lose or gain, to tell the truth and present the company, its people and opportunity in a fair and factual way.

Whatever you decide, I wish you the best of luck in this opportunity or any other in which you choose to pursue.

Steve Siebold
Bona Allen Mansion
Buford, Georgia
June 20, 2018

PART ONE

THE COMPANY

World Financial Group (WFG), formerly known as World Marketing Alliance (WMA), is a financial services marketing firm based in Johns Creek, Georgia. This organization and its senior leaders have been in business together for over 25 years. WFG uses a networking or multilevel marketing structure to recruit, train and compensate its 70,000+ independent licensed associates. WFG operates throughout the United States and Canada. The company's mission is "to help families from all walks of life build a solid financial future."

From left to right: Xuan Nguyen, Rich Thawley, Jack Linder, Jeff Miles, Tom Mathews

MY OPINION OF
THE COMPANY

World Financial Group is a mid-size company with a large independent sales force that's proven to be stable and successful over a long period of years. It operates in one of the most highly regulated industries in the world. The company has experienced its share of challenges, most notably the class action suit filed against it regarding the Transamerica Premiere Financial Foundation Indexed Universal Life Insurance Product it markets. Opponents claimed that the product was faulty due to the escalating cost of insurance as the policyholders aged. As a consultant to some of the world's largest companies, I can tell you that legal actions against them are not uncommon. As a matter of fact, the case could be made that much of the human resources profession is based on corporations attempting to prevent lawsuits and other legal actions. Legal action is commonplace in corporate America, and while in some cases the actions are legitimate, other times it's a matter of greed. Wealthy corporations are often the targets of disgruntled employees and greedy consumers looking to cash in. I've known each of the WFG presidents since 2006, and they are people of high standards and integrity. If I were a WFG associate, I would feel confident that the company was behind me every step of the way. Due to the entrepreneurial nature of the business, WFG corporate leaders and employees operate more like a family than a cold-hearted corporation. They take their jobs very seriously because they know how much the field counts on them. Over the years, I've known people who worked everywhere from the reception desk to the sales and marketing department, and they are a dedicated team.

Over the decades of consulting companies like Johnson & Johnson, GlaxoSmithKline and Toyota, I've worked with some of the strongest teams in corporate America. The feeling at WFG is different, and the difference lies in the culture and mission of the company. It's more than something they plaster on the wall at headquarters. You ask most employees what their company's mission is and you'll likely get a blank stare. At WFG, the mission is sacred, and if you ask, they are more than happy to share it with you.

So is WFG on its way to becoming a Fortune 500 goliath? As someone who helps large companies become larger, my guess is that WFG will continue to grow. Whether or not it becomes the next Apple Computer, only time will tell. In a way, I hope it doesn't. This company is big enough to help thousands of people with their money yet small enough to have a heart. WFG not only wants to make a profit; it wants its associates to win. In corporate America, that's not always the case. Many large companies treat their people like commodities and cogs in the wheel. They're a means to an end. WFG is small enough to care and large enough to count. Anyone who underestimates this doesn't understand the impact of a company's culture. When employees feel connected to a cause and they're able to work and grow in a positive, mission-driven culture, the switching costs of moving to another company tend to escalate. WFG is a place where its employees want to be.

THE PRESIDENT

Joe DiPaola, WFG's president for almost a decade, presides over this multimillion-dollar organization. Mr. DiPaola started his in- surance and financial services career as a field agent, branch man- ager and general agent. After running his own successful agency for 10 years, he joined Transamerica Life as senior vice president of TIIG's Western Regional Marketing Center in 2006. In 2009, he took over as president of World Financial Group.

MY OPINION OF THE PRESIDENT

Joe DiPaola is a class act. I liked him from the first time we met. He has a lifetime of experience in the insurance and financial services industry, and he's served as both a field and corporate leader. Joe's experience on the ground is a tremendous asset to the field leaders because he can relate to the unique challenges of this business model. I've seen him interact with hundreds of WFG associates, and he is both affable and down-to-earth. If there's a problem in WFG, he's the kind of leader you want representing you.

The WFG opportunity offers a wide range of choices, including part-time and full-time income opportunities that can potential- ly extend into six- and seven-figure annual incomes. Only a small percentage of associates reaches a $100,000+ income, with the average associate earning far less. Each associate starts in the same place and has the same opportunity to rise through the ranks regardless of background, education, politics or any other barrier that often blocks people from progressing in an organization. New associates sign an Associates Membership Agreement (AMA) and pay a fee of $100 USD to get started. In Canada the fee is $125 CDN. Additional life insurance licensing fees vary from state to state, with an average cost of several hundred dollars. Securities and advisory licensing fees are beyond that. Here are some recent income statistics from the company:

Leadership Level	Average Earnings	Highest Earnings
Senior Marketing Director (life licensed only)	$51,960	$592,460
Senior Marketing Director (life and securities only)	$63,721	$352,989
Senior Marketing Director (life, securities, and advisory)	$87,732	$1,612,669
Executive Marketing Director	$201,058	$1,347,137
CEO Marketing Director	$424,789	$2,311,962
Executive Vice Chairman & Up	$1,046,691	>$10,000,000

MY OPINION OF THE OPPORTUNITY

Financial literacy, life insurance and additional income are three things almost everyone needs. The World Financial Group opportunity is rooted in these critical components. The money that WFG associates earn is real. WFG pays out as much as $2 million each and every day to their field force. This opportunity, while shrouded in the haze of a controversial business-building model known as multilevel marketing, is not a scam or pyramid scheme. WFG offers a legitimate method of making money, and the top earners make a lot. The investment to get involved is minimal, and the upside potential is substantial. The WFG business model is both democratic and fair, and unlike climbing the corporate ladder, politics play no part in your potential success or failure. Everyone starts in the same place and has the same opportunity to rise through the ranks. Your success is not based on whom you know in the organization, where you went to school or your family's pedigree. WFG doesn't care if you have a PhD in physics or a GED from a reform school. All that's required to join this family of entrepreneurs is a clean background and the dream of a better life and the willingness to fight for it.

Do the leaders sometimes get overheated in the presentations and use hyperbole when describing the opportunities and bene- fits? Maybe, but no more than the thousands of pharmaceutical, technology and medical device salespeople I've trained. While hype rarely persuades people, it's usually the result of an excited associate who temporarily allowed his or her emotions to escalate. In all the years of observing WFG opportunity overviews (known as business presentation meetings), I've never seen a presenter purposely exaggerate the opportunity. These people are excited about their future, and they want you to become a part of their crusade to help families while helping themselves. Because the barrier to entry to become a WFG associate is so low, levels of education and sophistication vary greatly. You'll find leaders with doctorates from Johns Hopkins and high school dropouts from

Queens. The WFG field force is not a bastion of the elite. Rather than attracting the well-polished boxer, WFG more frequently attracts the scrappy street fighter with a lot of heart and little to lose. They pull from the masses of the US and Canada, mostly average people searching a way to break out and stake their claim. They don't expect special treatment or handouts, only a chance to fulfill their potential and escape the rat race. If these people had millions of dollars to purchase a McDonald's fran- chise or the education to become a corporate CEO, they probably would do so. WFG is a financial vehicle for the average person with the courage and ambition to break out of the masses.

People who attempt to delegitimize the WFG opportunity simply don't understand it. Anyone who understands even the rudimentary aspects of capitalism must respect the WFG opportunity because it represents the purest form of the concept. WFG associates help families with their finances that larger, more prestigious firms won't even talk to. When you're worth millions of dollars, the large financial firms love you. When you have $200 to your name, and you're in debt up to your eyeballs and can barely pay your bills, not so much. These are the families that WFG targets, both to help with their finances and to offer a way out of living paycheck to paycheck. The networking or multilevel compensation structure that people like to demonize has lifted many WFG associates out of financial disaster, and it's even made some of them wealthy. And be reminded that this money, whether in large or modest sums, wasn't handed to them or taken from others. They earned it, honestly and fairly, by serving others. Is that not the heart of what built this country? Is that not the very essence of capitalism, which has single-handedly created the greatest standard of living in the history of the world?

If you want to pick apart the problems of any networking style opportunity, you can. For example, the commissions on sales before you reach the senior marketing director level are low. You might earn higher commissions in a traditional company, but the initially low commissions are necessary in this structure to distribute the payout over multiple levels. It's not designed to shortchange the new associate but rather to compensate the people in the hierarchy who have contributed, either directly or indirectly, to the sale by building distribution. So while you could make more money in sales commissions with a traditional company to start, you wouldn't have the opportunity to recruit and build a team that offers you the potential for greater profits. Both models are solid; it just depends on what best suits your needs and personality style. The traditional life insurance salesperson must earn every penny he gets in linear fashion. If he doesn't work, he doesn't get paid beyond his residuals. In the WFG opportunity, the most successful associates earn money while they're sleeping due to the collective efforts of their team. In WFG, you work hard and earn less in the beginning, but once you become successful, you work less and earn more for the rest of your career. To me, it's a superior model, but you may see the larger up-front money as more attractive. If you're willing to commit to WFG as a serious lifetime career, I think you should consider joining them. If you're more interested in making a few bucks selling insurance as a side hustle, I'm not sure this opportunity is for you. I've met lots of what I call "WFG hobbyists" over the years. I've spoken to thousands of them at book signings, had hundreds of them call our office for advice, and received thousands of their emails. I always tell them the same thing: entrepreneurship is not a hobby. If you want a hobby, start a stamp collection. If you want to build a serious business with a large income, WFG or otherwise, you'd better be ready to make a lifetime commitment. WFG's biggest stars didn't build their businesses on a whim; they built them on commitment—year by year, month by month, week by week— failing a good portion of the time, learning as they struggled, and slowly eking out small successes that eventually grew to big successes. WFG is not a toy. If you're just looking for something to do, walk on by.

As obvious as this seems, the Internet contains thousands of posts written by disgruntled associates who failed and blame WFG. They rant and rave about how the wicked WFG forced them to join and then refused to build their business for them. They scream about WFG being a scam and a cult that coerced them into purchasing life insurance, made them go to meetings and encouraged them to harass their family and friends. I've read thousands of these complaints online over the course of many years, and the same thought always occurs to me: are these people adults or children? Did their leader force them to participate like a child being forced to attend school? After all, these are adults. On top of that, there are former associates who whine about being pressured to attend annual conventions in Las Vegas and elsewhere for their own development. It's like reading the irrational rantings of a child. Now, if by any chance any of these complaints seem valid, by all means do not join WFG. Because yes, the leaders will strongly encourage you to follow in their footsteps so you can succeed, which may include spending money you don't have to grow yourself and your business. People say that going into debt in order to start and grow your business is a bad idea, and I agree. It's always better to pay as you go. But what if you don't have the money to fly to conventions, attend personal development seminars, or invest in a good suit, business dress or other tools that are critical to the success of your business? What do you do then? Well, what most of us do… borrow it. We get loans from family or friends, or we finance it on a credit card. This is not the best way to start a business, but I promise you that in America, it's the most common way. I started my first business in 1987 when my wife and I were living on a very small income from our jobs. We didn't have any extra money, but Visa was willing to float us a few hundred dollars, albeit at 22% interest, but it was the only place that would. We ran up about $5,000 on that card, and the business failed. So we started another business and worked it hard for two years, and it failed. That put us at $11,000 in credit card debt at 22% interest, and we started going under every month. We were advised to focus on our jobs, work overtime for extra pay, and within five years we would be able to pay the $11,000 back with interest. My wife and I both knew this was solid financial advice, and by scaling back our unrealistic dreams of financial independence, we could find our way back to solvency. We agreed that it was the most prudent path to follow. But you know that old saying about how ships are safest in the harbor, yet that's not what ships are built for? Yeah, that saying kept waking us up at night. So instead of doing the smart thing and paying off debt, we came up with a new business idea and begged Visa to loan us another $5,000. Of course they declined, but eventually they grew weary and gave us $2,000. Our family financial planner said we were being fiscally irresponsible, and he was probably right.

My wife and I considered his advice, decided to ignore it, and bet the last $2,000 on ourselves—not to show or place, but to win. And over the next few years, we turned that $2,000 into a modest fortune.

I'm not suggesting you should borrow money. It's a risky proposition. I wouldn't even dream of asking you to put in the time and effort we invested to build our business. While our 20-something friends were partying, we were working nights, weekends and holidays. And we are not unique. This is what start-up entrepreneurs do, whether in WFG or any other business. That's the price you pay for success. You draw up a plan, fund it any way you can, and do whatever it takes to make it. You need only one big hit. One home run wins the game and effectively erases all the past failures. Granted, this life is not for everyone, but for some of us, it's our one and only chance for financial independence.

The advantages of the WFG opportunity are worth taking into consideration. First of all, the up-front investment is miniscule. The financial education you receive from the company is worth many times what you invest to get started, so even if you never receive a commission check, you'll still come out ahead. The knowledge you gain will help you secure your financial future, whether in WFG or elsewhere. Much of what you will learn is not taught in schools, and these are concepts and strategies that anyone who applies themselves can learn. In addition to benefiting personally from this inexpensive education, you'll be able to pass your newfound expertise on to family and friends.

Compared to other MLM opportunities, WFG stands strong. There are other solid companies in the network marketing space that you may want to consider. These companies offer compara- ble compensation and start-up costs, with products ranging from similar insurance products and financial instruments to an- ti-ag- ing products and energy drinks. I've attended thousands of op- portunity meetings and conventions with many of these compa- nies over the past 30 years, and while most have good intentions, they rarely stay in business more than 10 years. The MLM busi- ness model has a history of volatility, which is another example of what makes WFG special. This company has stood

16

the test of time, and that affords its associates a level of peace of mind that most MLMers will never have. The MLM industry is famous for company hopping, where top leaders build a massive hierarchy, cut a better deal with a competitor, and then attempt to convert their team to the new company. While this violates their contract and no one can be forced to switch companies, it happens, espe- cially to companies that don't care for their people. One of the things I've found most fascinating about WFG is I've seen this happen only a few times. In other companies, it's a standard as- pect of the business. In WFG, the associates are emotionally com- mitted and loyal to the company, their leaders and their teams in a way I've witnessed only on sports and military teams. The only way to actually fail is to quit. WFG is like a family no one wants to leave, even if they're struggling. When even the newest and lowest-ranking family member attains the most rudimentary rank, they're publicly celebrated, recognized and rewarded as though they had broken a world record. I've seen WFG awards ceremonies where people were awarded trophies so big they couldn't carry them off the stage. And it's occurred to me more than once that for these people, it's likely the most recognition they've ever received in their lives.

There's no doubt that this is a powerful business strategy. Anyone who has ever led a team knows that recognition is an important tool. But in WFG, it's more than that. It's the foundation of their culture. It's who these people are. It's easy for the skeptics to say that this company's culture is simply an associate retention strategy, and there's no question that it plays a part. But upon further examination, I can assure you that it's more than that. I've had a backstage pass to the WFG phenomenon for many years. As both one of the longest-serving vendors to the company and a friend and fan to many of its top leaders, I've been in the back rooms and witnessed the sausage being made. What I've seen more than anything are sincere, loving people doing their best to do the right thing. I recall a WFG event that I spoke at in 2006. I was scheduled to speak at 11:30 a.m., but the meeting was running behind, and I was asked to cut my time in order for the 10,000-person audience to adjourn for lunch at noon. I told the top leader who had invited me to speak that I wouldn't be able to deliver my complete Mental Toughness speech in 30 minutes.

He said:

> *"That's ok, Steve. I just want you to imagine the associate in the audience that's struggling and disheartened, and I want you to lift him up. Just speak from your heart about your experience with this company and what you've observed. If your speech inspires one person to keep going, you will have earned your fee."*

Now, I can tell you from over 20 years in the keynote speaking business that I've never had any client say that to me. In that moment, I realized that this company was about more than making money; they were about building people.

As the years went by and WFG continued to grow, I eventually realized the secret to their success wasn't the opportunity. While their compensation plan was solid and the potential earnings substantial, I'd seen similar compensation structures. The low start-up costs were certainly not to be overlooked, but I'd seen others that were even lower. The coaching and mentoring the leadership offered were great but not that different from the other companies for which I had worked. These are standard benefits of the MLM business model, and there are many good ones out there. After attending and speaking at hundreds of small and large meetings for WFG over 10 years, I finally uncovered the true north of their success: their culture.

Siebold on stage in San Jose, California with Field Leader Eric Olson

THE WFG CULTURE

As an author, speaker and consultant to Fortune 500 sales teams, I have over 20 years of experience with many of the largest corporate cultures in the world, ranging from nurturing to toxic. A company's culture can be defined by the way employees explain "the way it is around here." It's an ethereal concept, yet the emotion it evokes and the results it creates are real. How an organization makes its people feel is arguably its most important job because in a very real sense, the employee is as important as its customers. Companies that understand this develop and promote their people while companies that don't are forced to manage a revolving door.

WFG associates, while technically independent contractors, are treated in a unique way. This may be why it's sometimes accused of being a cult. I've watched hundreds of people attend WFG opportunity meetings, sign an AMA and immediately get treated like the next star in WFG. It's assumed that they will be successful, and the confidence this instills in the new associate is likely more than anyone has ever given them. I can assure you that WFG is not a cult but that it has a cultlike culture. And I mean that in the best sense of the term. As a matter of fact, there's an en- tire industry in corporate America dedicated to helping compa- nies develop, build and maintain a cultlike culture. Companies pay consultants millions of dollars to help them achieve this. The reasons are retention, productivity and profits. People who are emotionally connected to their company and coworkers work harder, produce more and rarely leave.

A perfect example is Simmons Mattress, who invested $10 million to transform its company into a cultlike culture. This three-year project was so successful it became a case study at Harvard Business School, and the company was later sold at a huge profit. I participated in some of these strategy sessions. But after seeing both of these cultures up close, I will tell you that WFG's is stronger…so strong, in fact, that even when an associate decides to leave WFG, the experience they have is so unique that it lasts with them forever.

I would describe WFG as a success culture. In other words, it's a culture that exudes, expresses and rewards everything related to success. Leaders aren't bashful about sharing their rags-to-riches stories or boasting of their big homes and lavish lifestyles. Most of these people come from humble beginnings, rise through the ranks and are proud of their accomplishments. Now, granted, this turns some people off. Some see this as self-aggrandizing or brag- gadocious, but in fact it's a key component of any success culture.

The educated observer may even view WFG as a microcosm of our American culture. Anyone who has traveled the world knows that there is no country more obsessed with success than the United States of America. The free enterprise system is based on our obsession with the American Dream. We're sold on this con- cept from childhood and fully expect to experience it. We want to win big, and we're willing to sacrifice to make it. This at- titude, point of view or philosophy, however you choose to label it, is uniquely American. That's not to say that there aren't mil- lions of highly ambitious people in other countries. But there is no other nation like America that worships at the altar of success. Fans of our obsession know it's what makes us special. It's why they risk their lives to escape to America. And in addition to the ones who have made it across our borders, millions have died in the attempt. That's how strong the appeal is to our success-ob- sessed, cultlike culture.

America is the greatest macroexample of this phenomenon. But as with any culture, not everyone likes it. America is criticized around the world for our obsession with hard work, success and thirst for wealth. Many believe we should work less and play more. They claim we don't understand that there's more to life than success. And on a microlevel, this is the same criticism that many lob at WFG. These people fail at the business, whine about it online and blame the opportunity for their failure. They rant and rave about how all the leaders talk about is success, and moan about how the most successful people get all of the atten- tion. Just as countries outside make the same claim about us, a percentage of failed WFG associates do the same. Since this book is designed to help you understand WFG, I won't take the time to make the case for the American way of life and our obsession with success. And while I proudly admit that it's true, I won't make a defense of it in this book. What I will say is that there's some validity in the claims of these failed associates. Does WFG recognize its champions more than the average associate? Yes, they do. And so does every major company, professional sports franchise and special military forces team. If you're looking for the "everyone gets a trophy" philosophy in WFG, you won't find it. Like the United States of America, WFG offers the opportunity to rise up and become somebody. It offers no guarantees, free rides or favoritism. What it does promise is that it will help you learn and grow every step of the way, and its leaders will cheer you on as you fight your way to success.

When immigrants come to New York and see the Statue of Liberty, they know it represents their chance for a better life. And on a microlevel, the WFG opportunity offers you the same thing in a more specific way. But as any immigrant will tell you, just showing up doesn't entitle you to anything. You must earn your bounty, and in WFG, you can earn a lot. Just don't expect something for nothing lest you be sadly disappointed.

While the WFG culture is success obsessed, it also has a big heart. I can't count the number of conversations I've had with leaders regarding their concerns for associates experiencing personal and professional struggles. WFG is a family, and this family looks after its own.

Are all of the leaders alike? No. Factions exist, as in any large organization. I witnessed the same thing during the seven years I consulted for Johnson & Johnson. Some leaders are more aggressive, and business-building philosophies vary from team to team. The company is full of big personalities and introverted leaders. Some are brash and bold, others quiet and humble. Like any large family, sometimes they get along, and other times they don't. I've seen this happen over the years as a trusted insider, and the impressive part is that they always come back together. No family is functional 100% of the time. But the most remarkable facet of this is how hard these people work to ensure that the family stays and grows together. The struggles I've seen with corporate teams are often the result of the leaders seeking a win-lose strategy in attempt to gain money, title or prestige. In WFG, the business model is win-win, and even in their disagreements, you get the feeling that family is looking out for family.

Now, if this cultlike culture turns you off, then WFG may not be for you. These people are intense competitors playing to win, and there's nothing casual about their culture. This is not a government job environment. These people are go-getters chasing financial independence, and they take no prisoners. They show up early, stay late, and dress for success. When you attend a WFG meeting, you know you're in a room with winners. They may be black, white, brown, Hispanic, Chinese, Indian, or Canadian, but psychologically, they're on the same path. Their dream is to be financially free, and they're willing to fight for it. They are the strivers, doers and dreamers, and they're in it to win it. This is not a game to them. In training sessions, you won't find WFG associates wearing flip-flops and t-shirts. You won't hear bad language or negative conversations because the associates are trained to think positively and focus their attention where it serves their best interests.

All I've ever seen in meetings and training sessions are associates hungry to win and eager to learn. They stand in line so they can sit in the front row. And if there are no seats left, they'll stand the entire meeting and take notes. It's impressive and inspiring. After standing on hundreds of stages over the years addressing WFG associates across the United States and Canada, I can tell you that the energy is palpable. It gives me hope for our capitalist system, with all of these ambitious young people fighting for their piece of the pie. I've never seen an audience take more notes or line up for a book signing. I've signed at least 50,000 books at WFG events, and the best part is the 30-second interactions I've had with people. They share their gratitude for the opportunity, their hopes and dreams for the future, and they're willingness to stay mentally tough. I'm hired to inspire them, but oftentimes I'm the one who leaves the meeting with tears in my eyes. There's something so moving about these people that it's hard not to be affected. As a public speaker, I've addressed close to a million people, so I'm used to assessing the energy of an audience. Any performer who's spent years on stage has an acute awareness of what an audience is thinking through their verbal and nonverbal responses. As you would expect, some audiences are better than others. WFG is different. To me, it feels as though they are absorb- ing every word and are ready to take action the minute they walk out the door. The intensity of the culture creates a kind of magic that's hard to describe, to the point that when people leave the company, I often wonder where they go. Why would you ever leave a family that trains, supports and mentors you? A family that genuinely wants you to succeed? And they'll do all of this for free, on speculation that you will become successful and they will be compensated by the company. It baffles me when people claim to have discovered a better way because after 30 years of doing business in 10 different countries, I've never seen anything like it.

HARD WORK

Some companies, especially in the tech space, encourage a light-hearted, casual work culture filled with ping-pong tables and video games. They believe in the idea that work should be fun so people want to stay. Maybe it's suitable and well designed for a less ambitious person. World Financial Group is old school. It's a loving, accepting culture that invites you to create your own future but never claims that the future you seek will come fast or easy. This is a company that prides itself on hard work, and it's evident in their success stories, from the Indian cab driver turned WFG millionaire to the college football star who parlayed his toughness into a WFG fortune. These are people who drank the Kool-Aid and turned it into liquid gold.

I've never met a leader in this company who brags about sitting under a palm tree, drinking out of a coconut. These people are workhorses who offer no apologies. The part-timers work their jobs all day and WFG all night, knowing that their hard work will eventually pay off. They pay the price now so they can enjoy the good life later.

If you're searching for an opportunity that promises wealth without work, forget WFG. But if you're not afraid to roll up your sleeves, you'll fit right in. These are not the sons and daughters of the rich; they are the products of hardworking people who passed on their world-class work ethic. If you're willing to follow their lead, they will work as hard for you as you do for yourself. There's nothing they respect more than hard work. But if you're lazy and looking for a free ride, they will respectfully leave you to your own devices.

POLITICAL LEANINGS

The WFG family is culturally, politically, ethnically and religiously inclusive. While seemingly pedestrian, this is not always the case in MLM. I've been to dozens of meetings in other companies that sound like old-time tent revivals. You won't see this here.

WFG associates tend to lean right. Liberals exist, but they are a minority. You'll find more people who believe in God, guns and grits than in a more left-leaning, progressive ideology.

WFG encompasses such a diverse culture that it's necessary to be politically and religiously neutral in order to include many different belief systems and ideologies. Many associates are new to North America from around the world. The organization has a strong Asian, Indian, and Hispanic contingent, and they are among the fastest builders in the company. I've seen other MLM companies with a similar mix of demographics, where the cultural infighting either destroyed or threatened the very foundation of the field force. What I've seen in WFG is acceptance and cooperation. The distinction with WFG is that despite their differences, the leaders know that it's in everyone's best interests to get along. The better the teams coexist, the more it benefits the collective
.

HEALTHY ENVIRONMENT

I would describe WFG as having a healthy environment that's rooted in learning and growing. You might even say that WFG is a personal development program disguised as a business opportunity. The leaders are vigorous advocates of entrepreneurism, self-education, and are constantly recommending books, seminars, videos, podcasts and improvement programs. When you walk into a WFG meeting, you are likely to be met with praise and pats on the back simply for showing up. You're guaranteed to leave the meeting feeling better than when you arrived. This is a place where people believe in one another, and not just because they are connected financially. I've been with groups that are unaffiliated, and they treat each other with the same respect and dignity. This pro-people climate runs far deeper than money and power. It's the very essence of the organization. Negativity and pessimism are quickly converted into their opposites. The associates are trained to have a winning attitude. The world-class atmosphere is contagious, and when a prospect enters a room full of associates, the energy is electric. I've stood on stages at WFG meetings and absorbed the energy coming from the crowd. It's like a tidal wave. It's very real, and its rooted in the excitement they feel about this business opportunity. WFG infuses real hope into their people's lives. Where before they may have been frustrated and bound by the limits of their background, education or experience, they now see their potential as limitless. That's a shift in consciousness that would excite even the toughest cynic, and it spills over into everything they do. WFG isn't just a business; it's a new lease on life. It's a chance to become the person you always knew you could be and a shot at living a fabulous lifestyle. I've had associates confide in me that WFG gave them their life back, offered them hope for a better future and made them feel like they mattered again. I've had them call my office and share things they were more comfortable explaining to a third party, knowing I had no formal connection to the company. They confide in me and ask for advice. And I tell them the truth, which is that most likely, this is going to be the best shot they ever get at the big time. I always hedge my comments by stating that I could be wrong, but the odds are that WFG will be your best shot. Not to mention being part of an uplifting, life-affirming group of people who are always in your corner cheering you on. I was in an office that has the words "Respect People, Make Money, Have Fun" on the wall in the boardroom. You can get one of those anywhere. You can get two at a few places. But to get all three is very rare. Where else are you going to find a chance at that?

WFG is not just a company; it's a community—a place where effort is rewarded, failure is fought, and success is celebrated. It's like a church without the religion that calls on the higher levels of people's nature. This community is built around free enterprise, helping families insure their financial future and success through financial independence. The members expect the very best from one another, and emotional support is offered in the form of tough love peppered with the empathy that can be offered only by a fellow striver.

What you won't find is self-pity, complaining and whining. All of these were purged from acceptability when the company first began. If you're looking for a shoulder to cry on, you won't find it here, but you will find comrades quick to encourage and slow to criticize.

The age demographics of the WFG community span the spectrum. There are 18-year-old associates and 70-year-old associates. The younger people have the energy, the older people the credibility, and sandwiched in between is the average associate. The beautiful part of this community is that no matter what the age, they all have one thing in common: they are fighting for financial freedom, a goal that only a small percentage of Americans and Canadians will ever achieve. It's a goal big enough to inspire and realistic enough to believe in. This dream is the glue that bonds the generations. And they never tire of talking and dreaming about it. They love to share WFG war stories with one another because despite their difference in age, they are all warriors fighting the same battle.

COMPETITION AND COOPERATION

Friendly competition is a part of the culture in many of WFG's hi- erarchies. Some of the leaders have athletic backgrounds, oth- ers are from the military and a sizable contingent is from the entre- preneurial and corporate sectors. As a former professional tennis player turned entrepreneur, I recognize the power of competition for certain personality types. Some people are driven to outper- form their WFG peers in income, speed and rank. I've watched WFG teams go head-to-head with other teams, elevating them all to levels of performance that they would not have otherwise achieved. In my years of observing these teams, I've never seen the competition escalate beyond the fun of competition among friends.

Many times in the middle of training a team, I've pulled out my cell phone on stage and dialed their biggest internal competitor. I have them hurtle friendly chants and challenges to the leader on the phone. Everyone high-fives, and the leaders enjoy a good laugh. It's all done in the spirit of fun, yet the competition is both healthy and real. Not all the groups actively embrace internal competition. Some seem to operate better by focusing on their own performance and aspiring to beat their own personal best. Every WFG team has its own style and dynamics, which makes the collective associates base that much more interesting when they come together

.

CELEBRATION AND RECOGNITION

After speaking at thousands of meetings and conventions around the world, I've seen my share of corporate celebrations, awards ceremonies and recognitions. Most large companies do a good job recognizing their people and rewarding their efforts. The first time I experienced a WFG awards banquet, I could have sworn I was watching the medal ceremony at the Olympic games. The first one I saw was in San Diego, around 2006, where the leaders were handing out four-foot-long metal swords in handsome leather cases. I had delivered our Mental Toughness University seminar to a group of 800 associates that day, and I decided to stay for the awards dinner that night. One by one, new associates were called to the stage, recognized for achieving a 90-day goal and presented with their trophy. These people were beaming with pride as they thanked the leaders and waved to their colleagues in the audience. The crowd came to its feet for each and every winner, and cheered as though each one had just broken the four-minute mile.

If this level of recognition had been given for a lifetime achievement, I would've understood. But when I asked the president of the company what it was for, he said, "This is for new people who hit their very first sales and recruiting goal." Being a wise guy, I replied, "Geez, what do you give them when they hit a big goal, a new car?" Without hesitation he said, "No, but pretty close." We both laughed, but I could tell he wasn't kidding. So I settled back in my seat and watched the parade of winners pridefully accept their awards and strut across the stage. And then out of nowhere, the emcee called my name. He said, "We want to thank Steve Siebold for coming all the way from Florida to coach us on mental toughness. Steve, please come up onstage." So I got up there, and the emcee shook my hand and said, "On behalf of WFG and our entire team, please accept this token of our appreciation." He then handed me a plaque with a photo of the 1980 Olympic hockey team on it with all the players' signatures. I was blown away. Then he gave me the microphone. I don't recall exactly what I said, but I remember looking at the audience and seeing all of these grateful, excited, happy faces. I knew in that moment that I was experiencing something special.

I quickly learned that celebration and recognition were a big part of WFG's culture, as well as part of its success formula. After all, who doesn't like to be recognized? I spend a lot of time on stages, but the way they gave me that award really moved me. Even though I was an outsider, they made me feel like part of the family. And they did it effortlessly. That's when I knew these people were professionals at this. Clearly, this was not an isolated event, and I was not the first outsider they had embraced and recognized. Over the next few months of speaking to their teams, I had a backstage pass to the WFG recognition machine, and to call it impressive is an understatement. I watched associates across the United States and Canada being celebrated while their WFG family cheered from the audience as if they had just hit the winning run in the World Series.

Most psychologists agree that no one, no matter how successful in life, has ever been sufficiently affirmed. We are all starving for personal affirmation, or just the basic positive recognition that all of us crave yet rarely receive. Most of us are reminded of our shortcomings on a regular basis from cradle to grave, and we hunger for anything or anyone who affirms our self-worth.

WFG has mastered this process. Of all the great organizations with whom I've worked, when it comes to celebration and recognition, WFG is the best. And that's saying something considering that I'm comparing them to companies that dwarf them in size. WFG isn't the biggest company, but when it comes to culture, they are the best. If you follow their system and rise through the ranks, you will receive more recognition than you ever have in your life. I guarantee it.

CAMARADERIE

When I was a competitive tennis player in the 1970s, one of the things I missed was being on a team. There's something special about winning as a team that's impossible to experience when you're representing only yourself. In 1974, I had the opportunity to play on a team representing the United States against the Australian junior team. For 12 months we trained for these two matches, one to be played in Chicago and the other in Sydney, Australia. What I enjoyed most was the camaraderie. Through all the hard work and sacrifice, a group of players who had been trained to compete as individuals came together as a team. There's a transformative power that's hard to explain when you're playing to win for a team. We fought harder for one another than we ever would have for ourselves.

WFG fosters a similar feeling. Every member of the team matters, and when you do well, it has a positive impact on everyone. You're in business for yourself but not by yourself. You have a team of people who not only want you to succeed; they need you to succeed. The business model is based on helping others get what they want, and when they do, everyone wins. And these people are not just coaches, like I had in tennis. They are stakeholders in your success. When you win, they win. It's a beautiful model because it leaves no one behind. The only way you can fail is if you quit or refuse to work.

I'll give you an example I experienced personally in WFG in 2017 and early 2018. It's an underdog story everyone loves, and the entire WFG family is reveling in it. A former taxicab driver and construction worker named Raja Dhaliwal, an Indian expat living in Edmonton, Alberta, Canada, who joined WFG in 2009 is a soft- spoken, fiercely driven man who left his family business in India to seek a better life in Canada. He was tired of the corruption in the old country and set his sights on Canada to stake his claim. He drove a cab to make ends meet and eventually entered the construction industry. But that wasn't enough for Dhaliwal. When I had dinner with him in Edmonton in February of 2018, he told me why. He said, "Steve, I didn't leave India and change

32

my entire life to settle. I wanted to do something big, and WFG gave me that chance."

The day in 2017 when the company announced that Raja Dhaliw- al had just hit $5 million in annual income, you could hear the WFG family cheering from Edmonton to Miami. Every WFG team I've spoken for across the United States and Canada has celebrated Raja's success. Most of these teams are not connected financially to Raja, but they are still part of the WFG family. I've never witnessed any jealously over Raja's success, only pride that one of their own had scaled another mountain.

What I've observed over the years with other stars of the company is similar in that when one wins, they all win. They are tied together like brothers and sisters, and the camaraderie between them is special.

THE MISSION

One of the driving forces in the WFG opportunity is their mission, as I mentioned earlier, which is "to help families from all walks of life build a solid financial future." Let's be honest; every company has a mission statement. It doesn't take much to assemble a committee and craft a mission statement. Unfortu- nately, that's where it often begins and ends. The mission state- ment is printed on a plaque, hung in the home office and forgotten.

At WFG, the mission statement motivates the field force as much as their quest for financial independence, but not for the reason many people think. At first glance, you might assume that their passion revolves around money, and for some, that may be true. WFG has over 70,000 associates, and I certainly can't speak for the collective. However, during the years that I've known these people, I've developed a theory.

As many of the top financial firms steer their associates away from serving low-and middle-income families to focus on helping the rich get richer, WFG sees opportunity. In fact, WFG has built their entire company around providing financial advice, tools, services and personal care available to the rich to every family regardless of income or net worth.

WFG associates don't target the super-rich or the top 1%. They know those families are well served. Instead, they focus on serving the families that can be overlooked by typical financial professionals, which is the middle and working class with little if any net worth. While this may appear to be an uninspiring market, it's the market segment that excites associates most. Why? My theory is that the WFG associate targets the little guy because he or she is the little guy. The average associate comes from the same socioeconomic class that's ignored, marginalized and left behind. They know what it is to be unwanted and invisible. Empowered by WFG, they go back for their brethren.

At a recent book signing for Xuan Nguyen's hierarchy in Atlanta, one associate confided in me, "Steve, I got into WFG to make money, but I'm staying in to save people from financial disaster. I know I can't save them all, but I can save some." I've heard various versions of this comment from associates across the company. Many of these people were themselves left behind. They feel like a cog in the wheel or a number on a corporate org chart. WFG restored their hope and optimism, and they want to share this gift with others. This mission extends beyond money and taps into the collective frustration that millions experience as a casualty of the American Dream.

Another motivator driving the field force is the aging population, struggling to retire without the funds necessary to live comfortably for the next 30 to 40 years. The majority of baby boomers, of which 10,000 are entering retirement age every day, are financially ill-equipped. Many will need to work until they die while millions of others will be physically unable and forced into poverty. WFG associates see their opportunity as a lifesaver and passionately promote it to this drowning demographic.

CORE VALUES

Every company makes a statement touting their core values. This is often done more for marketing purposes than it is for em-ployees. In the 1990s, I led a team of senior executives at Miller Brewing that crafted the core values and mission statement for the company. Anheuser-Busch, Miller's primary competitor, was crushing them, and senior management believed they could make a difference by clarifying their values to customers and stakeholders. We held a five-day session in Minneapolis, and the messaging of the company's values emerged clearly and concisely. The results were positive in both increased revenue and productivity.

I've consulted for numerous corporations on the architecture of communicating their core values. The difference is that WFG never needed a writer to craft theirs. The values that drive WFG are blatantly obvious to every associate. The entire business model, both the marketing of financial services and business op- portunity, is built upon helping people. Associates help clients, and leaders help associates learn to sell and build teams. Helping people is a foundational core value of WFG from both the corporate and field perspective. Here's how WFG's president and CEO describes it:

"Helping people is part of WFG's DNA. It's one of our core values and an integral part of our culture." - Joe DiPaola

Now, admittedly, WFG is not the first company to state that helping people is one of their core values. But after observing both the company's and field leadership's behavior over the course of many years, I've watched their actions back their words.

This integrity is on display every day at WFG, both at the home office and out in the field. Does this mean I haven't met people more out for themselves than others? Of course not. Like any organization, some leaders are better than others. The same is true at Microsoft, Procter & Gamble, Caterpillar, and every othermajor

35

company. The quality of leadership varies by personality. The difference I've seen with WFG is that the leaders are always pushing themselves to improve. This a breath of fresh air after working alongside hundreds of leaders in traditional companies satisfied with the status quo and counting the days until retire- ment. I've spent countless hours with WFG leaders listening to their concerns for new or struggling associates. Unlike many For- tune 500 leaders, these take responsibility for their team's success. I've witnessed the compassion they have for their teams. Once you spend time with these people, it's apparent that this opportunity means far more than the money. It's a life of helping people, and the more effective you are, the more you can earn.

Siebold with co-founder Tom Mathews on the front steps of the Bona Allen Mansion

THE PEOPLE

Over the past decade and a half, I've shaken hands, signed books and taken photos with literally thousands of WFG associates across North America, and it's in these 30-60-second blocks of interaction that I've developed a sense of who they are. I'm not talking about the WFG millionaires; I'm talking about the masses, the thousands of associates just getting started and the ones still hanging on.

These people are the heart of the hierarchies, and they're largely comprised of average people living common lives. They have spouses, mortgages and kids, and many enter the business with the goal of getting out of debt and making a few extra bucks. They represent a cross section of the US and Canada, and they have similar goals and dreams. Many have shared them with me, tears streaming down their hopeful faces. They've explained how they were lost in the daily grind, overwhelmed by work, raising kids and struggling to stay afloat. And then WFG came along. Most had never heard of this company but, after experiencing the presentation and people, had become swept up in a sea of newfound hope for the future. They share how the very idea of financial freedom drastically altered their outlook on life. They express their gratitude to their recruiter, the company and even their God for illuminating this opportunity. Being in their physical presence is moving. Their energy is electric, and their gratitude overflows like a waterfall on a warm summer day. It's been a privilege to interact with these people, however brief the encounter. They have been among of the most heartwarming of my career. Over the past 30 years of building businesses operating in 10 countries, I've met literally hundreds of thousands of people. In all that time, I've fallen in love with only one group, and that's WFG. The leaders have been extremely generous to me throughout the years, and the corporation has been a great customer. But it's the people of WFG that captured my heart, the ones who succeeded and the ones who quit, the people who made money and the ones still in the fight. These people are special. They have the courage to stake their reputations on a single turn of the wheel. They're not watching the game; they're in the game. Loved ones laugh and friends turn away, yet they forge ahead with little more than a dream in their heart and hope for the future.

THE VISION

World Financial Group wants to be the biggest and best in the industry, which is good but not uncommon for any corporation. It's what you'd expect. The more interesting vision comes from the field leaders, who love to compete and tout their team's success.

One leader who exemplifies this grand vision is Eric Olson. Olson is a former college football standout from San Jose State Univer- sity, who entered WFG as a student and built a thriving business. Olson is bold, brash and aggressive. At 6'5" and 300 pounds, he's an imposing figure with a personality to match. Now in his mid-thirties, he's one of the youngest superstars in the WFG stable. In 2017, I spent three hours in Olson's San Jose office exchanging ideas. When I asked him about his vision for the future, he told me his goal was to build the largest business in the history of the industry and to become a billionaire. When I pressed him as to why he wanted to become so wealthy, he said, "Because I know I can do it."

I was impressed that this relatively young man with limited life experience would be so daring. Upon witnessing his world-class work ethic and obsessive focus, you wouldn't want to bet against him anymore than you'd want to wrestle him. Olson's unabashed attitude matches his unbridled ambition. His no-prisoners approach may offend the town librarian, but for the young, hungry go-getter, it's a match made in heaven.

Another visionary of a different stripe is a woman named Penney Ooi. Hailing from Malaysia, she discovered WFG as a college student studying finance in the United States. Ooi has been with the company for nearly a quarter century and leads one of the largest teams in WFG. She runs the business with her husband Ben, a retired engineer also from Malaysia. Penney is smart, humble and an inspiration to her team. The Oois have earned millions in WFG and now seem even more motivated to help their leaders do the same. Ooi is a perfect example of a hungry, intelligent immigrant who rose from rags to riches. This is not someone who was born with a silver spoon. Penney Ooi fought her way to the top as a young female in a foreign land, and the team she leads is well aware of her hard work and dedication. I've seen her interact with her team over the years and found her to be one of the most sincere and compelling leaders in the field.

Olson and Ooi are just two examples of visionary field leaders who operate within the WFG organization, and both are successful and unique in their own right.

WFG seems to have a visionary leader to match every shape and style. While their visions and personalities vary, they share something in common. In order to fulfill their grandiose visions, they must help more people. It's the only road that leads to their dream. This means that thousands of present and future WFG hopefuls will have the once-in-a-lifetime opportunity to be mentored, coached and led, either directly or indirectly, by these powerful leaders. For the right person, it's a golden ticket.

THE HISTORY

World Financial Group has a long and storied history. Hubert Humphrey, Monte Holm, Jeff Miles and Rich Thawley were among the most successful associates at A. L. Williams in the 1980s. A. L. Williams was sold to Primerica in November 1989 and rebranded as Primerica Financial Services (PFS) in 1991. The four original leaders cofounded World Marketing Alliance (WMA) in December 1991. Jack Linder, Tom Mathews, Xuan Nguyen and Bryce Peterson came along soon after. In June 2001, selected assets of WMA were purchased by AEGON USA, and it was renamed World Financial Group (WFG) with the seven cofounders.

Hubert Humphrey moved on with a noncompete agreement.

Today, Holm, Mathews, Miles, Nguyen, Peterson and Thawley remain active in the company as well as thousands of others who have come along since.

Though Hubert Humphrey hasn't been part of this organization for almost two decades, his ambition and vision are mirrored in many of the leaders who still dominate today. I've met with Humphrey on a few occasions, once more notably in 2012. During this two-hour meeting, I witnessed the uniqueness and power of this once-dominant leader. Humphrey struck me as eccentric and ex- treme. Now in his mid-70s, his energy and passion for the in- dustry are strongly intact. There's no denying the massive shadow that Humphrey casts over this company, as well as the Business Format System that's become his legacy.

TRAINING

Of all the companies for which I've worked, WFG provides more real-world, hands-on training than any of them. Even the famed pharmaceutical companies, which are well-known for world-class training, don't hold a candle to WFG's comprehensive learning experience. Pharmaceutical companies invest up to $300,000 per salesperson, training them how to persuade physicians to prescribe their drugs. I've played an integral role in hundreds of these training sessions, and they are the most effective in the Fortune 500. But WFG takes training to a different level, where you have a personal mentor who guides your every move for as many years necessary at no cost. And unlike many organizations in corporate America, the mentor's compensation is tied directly to their charges' success.

The caring culture of a company is arguably the most overused, underdelivered claim that organizations make. It's a nice idea, it's politically correct, yet it's rarely practiced. This is not to say that most companies don't care about their people, but over decades of observing corporate cultures, I've seen only a few that live up to this claim. And then there's WFG, a company that's very existence relies on people caring about others. It's not that WFG is morally or ethically superior; it's that its business model demands that you educate, inspire and coach your recruits to become successful.

Granted, not everyone does this. Eighty percent of the people who sign an associate agreement (AMA) and pay the $100 fee are inactive within 12 months. Within 18 months, over 90% are gone. But the people who persist and succeed have helped hundreds improve their lives.

In addition to the collaborative nature of the business model, I would also argue that WFG attracts a certain type of person. As one executive vice chairman, Jun Dela Cruz, shared with me, "People who want to become billionaires are not typically attracted to WFG. This is a business of helping people get what they want, not just what you want."

I would agree with Jun 100%. Since 1984, I've interviewed over 1,300 self-made millionaires and billionaires. I wrote a book about my experience called How Rich People Think. In 2018, I penned another book called Secrets Self-Made Millionaires Teach Their Kids. So I think I can speak with some authority regarding the mindset of the rich. The people who care only about money I refer to as the killers. All they see are numbers, and they treat people like commodities. When I've asked them over the years how much money is enough, the most common answer is "more."

In all the years of meeting WFG associates, I've met only a handful of killers, most of whom were either terminated by the company or left before they got kicked out. These people made exaggerated claims and employed hard sell tactics. They're no different from the killers I've interviewed on Wall Street, who naively believe that money and material possessions are the keys to happiness. This mindset led them to break rules and attempt to win at all costs. And I'll be honest: on Wall Street, and even on Main Street, I've seen some of them get away with it, the ones I know are miserable even as they fly around on their private jets while hobnobbing with movie stars and sports heroes. The times I've spent interviewing these people at their homes in Aspen, Palm Beach, Martha's Vineyard and other haunts of the rich, I couldn't wait to get away from them. These people won the battle but lost the war. Many have been divorced multiple times, have drinking or drug problems, and are absolutely confounded that despite being masters of the universe, they are lonely and depressed. If you've never had an excess of money, this may be hard to fathom. If you've ever dined at an all-you-can-eat buffet, you can understand their mindset. Imagine getting stuffed at the buffet, yet you believe that eating more is better, so you continue gorging. Eventually the excess food begins to make you feel sick, yet you keep eating, believing that more is better.

This is stupid. No one with common sense eats himself sick. But when it comes to money, the killer is motivated by more, thinking it will ease his loneliness and lack of self-esteem. The stronger the belief, the more ruthless his moneymaking tactics. Eventually he either crosses the line, breaks the law or behaves unethically. Usually it's not too long before this naive mindset catches up. The problem is that once the killer reaches this point, his enormous ego obstructs him from identifying the true cause of his self-destruction.

My point is that the killer mindset doesn't play in WFG, and when someone who possesses it slips through the cracks, it's usually short lived. The mindset that WFG attracts seems to be one that aspires to be financially independent and wants to do it the right way. These people thrive on the idea that to become successful, they must help others along the way. In all my experience in business, I've never met more sincere, honest and genuine people than I have in WFG. This business model seems to bring out the best in people. I'm not trying to paint a picture of

perfection, nor am I suggesting that WFG is a capitalistic uto-
pia. I'm simply try- ing to make the point that it seems to attract
the most loving, car- ing creatures, the most successful of whom
make a lot of money, help a lot of people and have fun. If that
appeals to you, WFG may be a fit.

PERSONAL DEVELOPMENT

Fradel Barber, one of WFG's youngest and most successful female
associates, calls WFG "a personal development program with a
massive compensation structure attached to it." It's hard to argue
that the foundation of WFG's phenomenal success is rooted in
the organizations deep commitment to helping people grow personally and professionally. During a recent interview I conducted
with Barber at our headquarters, at the Bona Allen Mansion, near
Atlanta, I asked her the secret of her success. She said that prior
to joining WFG at the tender age of 20, she was very shy. Through
the encouragement of her WFG mentors, she immersed herself
in personal development and it changed her life. She went on to
earn over $100,000 in her first year with the company, and has
earned millions in the 14-years since.

I can attest to Barber's claim that WFG is an avid purveyor of
personal development since that's how I was first introduced to
the company. My first book, 177 Mental Toughness Secrets of the
World Class, came out in 2005. Ed Mylett, one of WFG's stars,
liked the book and began promoting it to the other WFG leaders.
Soon after, I was asked to speak at their training sessions across
the country. I had spoken for dozens of MLM companies in the
past, but our core clients have always been traditional corporate
sales teams. Speaking to the WFG teams was like coming home.
In traditional companies, I spend most of the time onstage attempting to convince salespeople that personal development is
the secret to success, and it's always an uphill battle. Since WFG
teams are trained to embrace personal development, they have
the entrepreneurial savvy to seek coaching. From the first team
I addressed, it was obvious that I was in the right place. I felt a

kinship with the associates that I had never experienced. I went from signing 20 books at Barnes and Noble to signing 500 books at WFG meetings. And I knew that it wasn't about me, it was about *them*. This is their culture.

Though I'm not a WFG associate, we are kindred spirits, and our connection begins with our shared belief in personal growth. If you believe that you're responsible for your own results in life, you'll likely love this aspect of WFG. If you're not sure about it, I suggest you give them a chance to persuade you. If any system can do that, it's WFG. It's not something they splash on their website or wear on their sleeve. This is something they truly believe in, and they're willing to bet their future on it. In WFG, personal development is deployed in conjunction with what associates do in the field. They don't just study books; they prospect, recruit and serve clients. They don't just talk a good game; they make things happen. Then they go home, wipe off the blood, and the next day they do it again. At night, before they drift off to sleep, they're studying the latest personal development tome and taking notes. This reenergizes them and prepares them for the next battle.

On Saturdays, they're often sitting in seminars, searching for one little edge that could put them over the top. This struggle is waged for months and sometimes years. Oftentimes the only thing keeping their dream alive is the promise offered in personal development. Eventually, their skills become strong and their minds even stronger, and the series of breaks they've been fighting for begin to unfold. The money starts to flow, and for some, it gushes. Once this occurs, they take their rightful place onstage among the company's elite performers. They feel the satisfaction of a well-fought victory. Deep down, they know they've earned the right to be standing in the victory lane. Their success is the re- sult of their efforts, but their ability to sustain those efforts comes from the growth they experienced through personal development.

The vast majority of critics who knock World Financial Group seem to be disgruntled associates who failed at the opportunity. You can read hundreds of pages online citing petty gripes against the company, opportunity and business model. That's not to say there aren't some legitimate complaints, but after months of research, I found very few. Complaints of hard-sell tactics, hyped-up presentation meetings and ego-driven leaders may hold a measure of truth. After all, with over 70,000 licensed associates, you're bound to see a variety of personalities and approaches. The company diligently monitors the field force to ensure the ethics and accuracy of the opportunity. In my experience, these complaints represent isolated incidences and do not accurately represent the WFG experience. But in the interest of full disclosure, let's explore them one by one.

Siebold and Field Leader Jeff Levitan on the front steps of the Bona Allen Mansion

HARD SELL TACTICS

Over my 13 years of attending BPMs, training sessions, internal meetings at the company's headquarters and one-on-one presentations, I've experienced a handful of times when leaders employed what some would call the hard sell. The hard-sell situations I've experienced were more about the excitement of a new presenter than the coercion of the audience. I've never seen a leader attempt to push a prospect to sign up. His or her excitement may have come across as a hard sell, but as a professional speaker, I can tell you that there's a thin line between being excited and pressuring an audience to buy. In the field of professional speaking, I've been labeled the "Opie Taylor" of the industry. If you're old enough to remember or you've seen the reruns, Opie was Andy Taylor's son on The Andy Griffith Show. Opie was the most honest of TV characters, and that's the reference some people in the speaking profession have linked to me. It sounds like a compliment, but it's meant as a criticism. Many presenters make millions of dollars using hard-sell and manipulative tactics onstage, and I refuse to do that. I didn't become a speaker to pressure people to buy things; I became a speaker to share what I've learned. Admittedly, I've had moments onstage when I've allowed my excitement for a product or service to overwhelm me to the point where one might interpret my presentation as a hard sell. This is the same thing I've seen in WFG, albeit very few times. In this area, WFG is not an outlier. I've delivered speeches and seminars to some of the largest companies in the world. I've trained over 25,000 pharmaceutical sales reps and managers in mental toughness, and I've ridden with dozens of them on sales calls to physicians across the country. These salespeople, like WFG associates, are among the most passionate I've ever encountered. They are very well educated in the prescription drugs they represent, and their conviction is unmistakable during their presentations. The doctors make them wait in the lobby, sometimes for hours, to see them, and once they do, they often refuse to even make eye contact with the reps as they are presenting their clinical data. It's borderline disrespectful of the doctors, but the reps remain undeterred.

I have never seen a WFG presentation that was even close to the hard-sell strategies employed by pharmaceutical sales reps. In their defense, if the rep failed to use these strategies, the doctors wouldn't even hear their presentation. The majority of WFG presentations I've experienced have been education-based and focused on the financial plight of the average person. These people are pumped up about the hope that's been restored in their lives, and they want you to see what they see. If they cross the line from excitement to hard sell in the process from time to time, I chalk it up as a harmless mistake.

I spent two years speaking on stages with TV evangelists, and if you want to see a hard sell, that's where you'll find it. Although I rarely agreed with their beliefs or tactics, I respected their passion. Some were more interested in money than saving souls, but most were there to help people. WFG presentations aren't even in the same category when it comes to pushing an audience. These pastors will cry, laugh, ridicule, insult and do almost anything else to get the audience to take action. This is not what you'll find at World Financial Group.

If hard selling is standard operating procedure in the office where you attended the presentation, I would find a different office.

FELLER ET AL VERSUS TRANSAMERICA LIFE INSURANCE COMPANY

In 2016, a class-action lawsuit was filed against Transamerica Life Insurance Company. The suit was related to raising the cost of insurance on some universal life insurance contracts, an action that plaintiffs alleged constituted a breach of obligation under the policies and led to damages against contract holders. Plaintiffs alleged Transamerica raised monthly charges by 38% and that they falsely stated the firm's increases were permissible under specific terms of the policies when they were actually to subsidize its cost of meeting its interest guarantee to recoup past losses on the policies and on its investment portfolio, and to make the policies more profitable by inducing policy terminations by those policyholders who could not afford the increase. The case was settled in 2017 in Transamerica's favor.

Critics of World Financial Group and its parent company, Transamerica, sometimes cite pending and past legal actions as a reason to denigrate the opportunity. The truth is that large companies are frequent targets of legal actions, which is why they have legal departments. I can't recall a single Fortune 500 client that wasn't in a constant battle with frivolous lawsuits. A few years ago, one of my clients was fined $3 billion by the United States De- part- ment of Justice for alleged activities that I know were untrue. I was intimately involved in this process, and I can state unequivocally that my client was innocent. They settled the case because it would have cost them a fortune in time and treasure to fight it. This case is an indictment of a legal system whereby anyone can claim anything and attempt to cash in. WFG has suffered similar attacks, and in some cases they've been forced to pay fines. Every organization makes mistakes, and when they do, they must make amends. If you have concerns about any past legal issues with the company, I recommend that you find out the truth of what really occurred in each instance. It's easy to find guilt, but uncovering the truth requires diligence. In the research I've conducted over the course of several months, I'm comfortable stating that WFG is an ethical company that operates under the highest standards.

THE MULTI-LEVEL
NETWORK MARKETING
INDUSTRY

MLM is one of the most controversial industries, mostly because people don't understand it and partly due to its abuses: front-loading people with thousands of dollars in physical products, selling only to downline distributors and making money on training tools instead of actual products, etc.

The biggest claim against MLM companies is that they are pyramid schemes, illegal financial arrangements in which paying participants recruit others with returns being given to early participants using money contributed by later ones. Pyramid schemes are illegal, and they should be. They are similar to Ponzi schemes in that they're an exchange of money with no product, service or enterprise attached to them. In the end, someone has to lose. Think of Bernie Madoff. I have dozens of friends in Palm Beach who lost millions with Madoff. One of my neighbors invested his entire life savings and committed suicide after Madoff's arrest. Ponzi and pyramid schemes are dangerous and unethical, but multilevel marketing is neither. I have years of experience working with MLMs and even launched my own several years ago. The premise is simple: you enroll in an MLM company to become an associate or distributor, and you develop customers or clients and sell to them for commissions. You also have the opportunity to recruit people to become associates/distributors, and in exchange for training them, you receive overrides on their sales. The bigger your team, the larger your overrides.

In legitimate MLMs like WFG, you don't get paid to recruit people, but recruiting is the most profitable part of the puzzle because of the potential overrides. The problem occurs when the MLM associate or distributor fails to develop retail customers or clients outside of the company's hierarchy. This happens in many MLMs, where it's essentially a wholesale buying club as opposed to a retail business model. This is not the case with WFG. Yes, associates are encouraged to purchase insurance contracts and other financial products if they are suitable, but they invest the majority of their effort in selling and recruiting people outside the hierarchy. WFG is a legitimate business model with both wholesale and retail clients.

If you want to sell life insurance as a career, join a traditional company with high commissions. The upside is you'll make more money up front, two to three times as much as you would selling through WFG. If you want to build a team of agents whereby eventually the bulk of your income could be generated through overrides, consider joining WFG. The additional benefit is that the overrides can be residual, assuming that your team continues to produce results. The term "residual income" is sometimes thrown around as though it's a guaranteed result, but if your team doesn't continue to produce, there are no team residuals. Residual income is an attractive concept, but it's based on your team's ability to perform. Financial products can be an exception. Some products pay compensation beyond the first year, so that could be considered residual income.

The last thing I'll ask you to consider regarding the MLM aspect of WFG is that it's arguably the most misunderstood aspect of the opportunity. Many people believe they understand the concept, but in 25 years of working with MLM companies, I've found that very few people have a solid grasp of how it actually works. I recommend that you study it carefully. The more you study, the more you'll appreciate its level playing field. I see it as the little guys' best chance to get ahead, and in some cases, the little guys get big. Only a small percentage build it, but why couldn't that be you? I've coached hundreds of big leaders in MLM, and they're no smarter than the average person. They may be more ambitious, hardworking and focused, but they're no smarter. If you apply yourself and follow the WFG system, you have a legitimate shot at making it big. No guarantees, but you've got a shot.

THE HYPE

Like many moneymaking opportunities, you may experience hyperbole at WFG business presentation meetings, training and conventions. The truth is that with a field force of over 70,000 associates, it's impossible for any organization to monitor every word that is uttered during the thousands of meetings that occur every day across North America. After attending MLM meetings representing over 100 different companies over the past 25 years, I've rarely experienced one that didn't involve a little hype. For- tune 500 sales teams are guilty of the same charge. Sales pre- sentations of all stripes are known for puffing up products. As consumers, we're adept at cutting through puffery. Many MLM companies need to add hype because they have so few people earning money, yet this is not the case with World Financial Group. Although it's a small percentage of associates, there are lots of people earning fabulous incomes in WFG. And there's a smaller group making very large amounts. This company is not only in the business of helping clients protect and grow their money; it's also in the business of creating millionaires, not to mention the sizable number of associates earning between $50,000 and $100,000 per year. WFG doesn't need to engage in hyperbole because it's producing successful associates. I've been to their homes, travelled, dined and delivered speeches with them, and I can assure you that this is no show.

THE PROS

The pros of joining WFG are numerous. No matter what you ultimately decide to do, this is a serious opportunity worth every minute you invest in its evaluation. The overall education you'll receive is worth many times the price of admission. You'll learn lessons in financial literacy, team-building, personal development and sales. You'll make dozens of friends almost overnight who are among the brightest and most ambitious people you'll ever encounter. These are people who are going somewhere in life, and being around them is an inspiration. You'll learn how to think big and take action to transform your dreams into reality. You'll become a member of a team that celebrates one another's successes and supports one another through disappointment and failure. WFG is a family, and though not related by blood, you wouldn't know it by observation. As a long-standing vendor to the company, I am technically not a member of this family, yet they've always treated me as such. No one discriminates against me for not being an associate. The leaders, from the president through the highest ranks of the field force, have always treated me as if I were a part of the team. And that's over a 13-year period. That says an awful lot about these people and the way they think. In traditional companies, even the ones with which we've had seven-figure multiyear contracts, I've never felt at home with them like I do with WFG. I believe you'll feel the same way because that's the culture of the company and why it thrives.

I believe with all my heart that if you decide to become an associate with this company, it will be one of the greatest experiences of your life. Someone said this to me about Amway back in 1984, and even though I didn't earn much money, the experience was unforgettable. After college and a short stint on the pro tennis tour, I decided on a career in coaching instead of continuing with Amway. But I'll never forgot the lessons I learned from Amway, something I've shared with Rich Devos, the cofounder, many times when we've crossed paths throughout the years on the speaking circuit.

What Amway offered back then is not in the same league as what WFG offers today. The chance to spend your life with winners chasing your dreams is something very special, something that few people even know exists, much less have the opportunity to experience. As a lifelong entrepreneur, I've had business partnerships, joint ventures and sole proprietorships. Along this 30-year journey, I've been fortunate to have more successes than failures. But the one thing I was never able to recreate is the very thing that WFG offers: teammates, a team of people with similar goals and dreams who are willing to take to the street and fight for what they want. There's a kind of magic in that. To me, that may be the biggest benefit of joining the WFG family. Being surrounded by successful people and those who aspire to be successful is an energy in which you can bathe. It will spur you on, knowing that you're not alone in your quest for the good life and that others are dreaming the same dreams. It's been said that there's power in numbers, and I think that the WFG family proves that. Succeeding alone is fine, but winning with a team has a sweetness unlike any other. The shared excitement, laughter, motivation, heartache, inspiration and struggle simply cannot be matched by any sole operator.

So as you can see, the pros are substantial. There is so much to be gained. That being said, every opportunity has downsides, or cons. So in the spirit of objectivity and fairness, let's explore them.

THE CONS

During my six months of in-depth research for this book, one of the questions I asked every leader was, "What's the downside of WFG?" Interestingly enough, not a single one of them had a problem listing the possible cons of their opportunity. The most common answer was hard work, especially in the first couple of years when the hours are long and the results are short. To be accurate, this is the experience the majority of people have but not all. Some associates buckle down immediately, get licensed quickly and earn a full-time income their first year. These results are rare, but they do happen. I know because I've seen people do this all over the United States and Canada. They attend my seminars and book signings and share their success stories. But odds are it's going to be ugly in the beginning, just as it is for most entrepreneurs. Start-ups, even turnkey businesses like WFG with a proven step-by-step system, can be a slog. It's an exercise in patience and persistence.

Another downside is that you'll likely be forced out of your comfort zone. This can be emotionally taxing, especially if you are shy, timid and addicted to the approval of others. In this business, it's likely that people are going to reject you over and over before you break through. Some may even laugh at you and your crazy dream of financial independence. When this happens with strangers, it's uncomfortable. When it happens with friends, it's painful. When it happens with family, it can be devastating. Many associates have shared their rejection stories and the emotional fallout they experienced. Sometimes it's hard for WFG associates to believe that their loved ones can't see the vision and opportunity. This is a downside for which you must be mentally prepared.

The sheer number of hours you'll need to invest in this business to become successful is a challenge for many people. This opportunity requires a measure of short-term sacrifice before the payoff. Many people are searching for instant gratification, and that rarely occurs in business. Whether you're planning on working WFG full or part time, plan on investing twice as many hours as

54

you think you'll need to launch. This has nothing to do with the WFG opportunity; it's just solid business-planning advice. As an entrepreneur who's launched dozens of start-ups, I can state with some authority that they almost always require far more time to get off the ground than what's stated in your business plan.

Plan on being bad in the beginning, knowing that someday you will be good. This can be difficult for people who have developed a high level of expertise in other fields and are accustomed to knowing the answers. WFG is a different animal. As simple as it may seem, I've looked behind the curtain. These leaders didn't get to where they are through luck; they got there through skill. The more time you spend with the top dogs, the more you'll discover their genius. As CEO Marketing Director James Schwartz told me, "I just submitted to the system. I didn't fight it or attempt to recreate it. I just followed it."

James was a military leader for many years, and he said that his experience helped him to follow the WFG system. Following WFG's Business Format System may be more challenging for creative personality types or others who struggle with control issues.

An additional downside to consider is the criticism that WFG gets online, as I detailed earlier. Any company that recruits 100,000 people a year with an 80% attrition rate is bound to have people who want to punish the company for their personal failure. When you read these threads, this is obvious, but the downside is that a percentage of people believe everything they read online. This will cost you a few recruits who can't get past the ranting's, no matter how silly or untrue.

Every opportunity has its share of cons or downsides, and WFG is no exception. Your job is to carefully evaluate the pros and cons and see which side wins. One of my key takeaways gleaned from the 107 interviews I conducted came from the field leaders. When I asked them what they would say to someone on the fence about joining, many suggested "give it a try." They said, "You won't know if it is for you until you try. After all, the investment is only the cost of a nice dinner in a decent restaurant. If you give it a shot and decide that the cons outweigh the pros, take what you've learned and the friends you've made and move on. On the other hand, if you decide that the pros are worth enduring the obstacles, you may have just discovered the opportunity for which you've been searching."

On a personal note, like most entrepreneurs, I'm not a big gambler. I like sure things and calculated risks. That's how you stay in business for 30 years. In the interest of full disclosure, I'm a proponent of this opportunity. If you've read this far, you already know that. Keeping my pro-WFG bias in mind, I ask you to consider the minor risk you'd be taking by giving this business a shot compared to the potentially large payoff. No matter how you analyze it, the math works. WFG is a calculated risk. Your downside exposure is nearly nonexistent while your upside potential is substantial. These kinds of bets are every entrepreneur's dream, and I can assure you from personal experience that they are very difficult to come by. My job, dear reader, is not to attempt to persuade you but to inform you. I only ask that you factor these thoughts into your decision-making process.

THE INVESTMENT

The financial investment to become a WFG associate is $100 USD or $125 CDN. None of this money goes to the person who recruits you. The money goes to World Financial Group and is used to pay for a background check, processing, and other expenses related to adding a new associate. Since WFG is simply a marketing platform that doesn't sell anything, this money is necessary to pay the staff and keep the lights on.

Getting licensed varies from state to state, but I would budget several hundred dollars. Less than 10% of associates ever gets licensed, but to make serious money, you'll need to be at least life-licensed. You'll also be advised to attend the Convention of Champions, usually held in Las Vegas during the summer. Tickets to this event are around $150, and approximately 35,000 people attend every year. I would strongly recommend that you attend this event every year and build it into your budget. Don't forget airfare, hotel, meals and miscellaneous expenses. You won't have much time to lose money in the casinos. This meeting is power-packed with information, education and motivation. You'll see and meet members of the WFG family from all walks of life, and their rags-to-riches stories will both motivate and move you. You need to attend this event for the leaders to take you seriously. Associates who don't attend are sometimes marginalized and not seen as future potential leaders. This is not done out of malice but out of necessity. Once you attend, you will understand. This is where people see the big picture and how they fit into it.

In addition to the annual convention, there will be Saturday meetings and personal development seminars for which you will need to purchase tickets. You may even see yours truly speaking at some of these events as well as other outside speakers and corporate executives from the company. Most of these events are low cost, but you should build them into your budget. Remem- ber that these events are not just for you; they are also for your team. If you, the leader, don't show up, your team will follow suit.

Other investments may include some nice business clothes and shoes if you don't already have them. A big part of what makes the WFG culture so professional is the way the associates dress for success. These people are serious about winning, and they are coached to dress for the part. That doesn't mean you have to invest in Italian suits and designer shoes; you just have to look professional at all times.

Compared to starting a traditional business, the up-front financial investment in WFG is ridiculously low. For a nominal start-up cost, you can launch a business capable of creating millions of dollars in commissions. With a few good initial sales, you'll be operating in the black.

THE HEADQUARTERS

World Financial Group is headquartered in Johns Creek, Georgia, a wealthy suburb located approximately 30 miles northeast of Atlanta. The company employs about 500 people. This 100,000-square-foot office building is stately and impressive, and the halls are lined with portraits of the stars in the field force. The building includes a prestigious theatre that seats about 300 people for trainings and meetings. If you're seriously considering becoming an associate, put a visit to the headquarters on your short list. Ask the person who recruited you what you would need to do to get a tour of the building. It's certainly not a requirement, but if you're going to pour your energy into this business, I would recommend that you visit the mother ship at some point in the near future. You won't be disappointed. This company is serious about helping their people, and they've invested an enormous amount of money in this world-class facility.

The headquarters is important because the savvy people you're going to recruit will want to know that this is a credible enterprise, especially since it's an MLM. While it's a brilliant business model, MLM has a poor reputation, much like the used car industry. The average consumer is unable to distinguish the good ones from the bad ones. The opulent building lends credibility the concept and the company. Your prospects will go online to conduct research, and they'll be impressed when they see the picture of the headquarters. Besides housing a knowledgeable and friendly staff, it serves as an additional marketing tool at no additional expense.

WFG co-founder and Past President Monte Holm onstage in Las Vegas, Nevada at the Convention of Champions

PART TWO

Pictured top to bottom, left to right: Team Pinnacle Leaders: Juan Jaime, Paul Hart, Eric Olson, Veronica Jaime, Gabie Hart, Sandra Olson

WFG STARS

WFG is a company chock-full of star associates who kicked and scratched their way to the highest ranks of the hierarchy. I've been privileged to get to know many of them. Like any large group, they are a cast of characters who range from wild extroverts to studious bookworms. Despite their differences, they have at least one thing in common: they all started their WFG business at the same level, the bottom, and worked their way up. No one bought their way to stardom or was handed their status. They all worked long hours for little pay and stayed mentally tough long enough to build a big team and serve a lot of people. This is one of the reasons I respect them. They fought for every rank attained and every penny earned.

Any attempt to paint these people with a broad brush would be an abysmal failure. Instead, I'm going present a cross section of associates who beat the odds. I won't be able to introduce you to all of them, but the people I've profiled will give you a feel for who they are collectively. In each profile, I've injected some personal opinions and reflections, which don't represent the company or anyone outside of myself. The purpose of my personal analysis is to give you a head start on your own evaluation.

The stars are presented in alphabetical order.

Fradel Barber

FRADEL BARBER

Fradel Barber was born and raised in Brooklyn, New York, one of 12 children. Her parents did everything they could, but with that size family, it was never enough. Fradel dreamed that one day she would become a successful fashion designer, and at 20 years of age, she headed from New York to California to pursue her degree. She had purchased a used car, which was waiting at Los Angeles International Airport when she arrived. This was her first time on her own and her first car. Fradel explains:

> *"I didn't know you had to put oil in a car, so after 30-days, I had no car."*

It wasn't the start for which she had hoped. But New Yorkers are known for being tough, and Barber is no exception. She had no car, no place to live and little money. She had prepaid for her first semester of school, but she desperately needed a job. She responded to an ad in the newspaper, got an interview and saw the WFG presentation. She was hooked from the start. During our interview, she gushed:

> *"I learned so much about money", she gushed during our interview. "So I signed up."*

As her first day of fashion design school was approaching, she began asking herself if she really wanted to pursue her previous- ly chosen path, or would she be better off going full blast with WFG? She eventually decided to plant her flag and go full time with the company. It was a decision that would drastically alter the 20-year-old's life, and eventually the lives of thousands of oth- ers over the next decade and a half. Barber's start in the business would make even the toughest New Yorker proud. She explains:

"I made six figures my first year. I sat down, put together a plan to make $100,000 a year, and then followed it."

Seems simple enough, right? Simple, but not easy. She continues:

"I self-analyzed. When I failed, I tried to figure out what I did wrong."

I asked her why she chose WFG over being a fashion designer:

"It was the money and lifestyle. I never dreamed of being in financial services. The first thing I noticed was that my own family never had this education. My dad worked for a corporation for many years and didn't have a retirement plan. He didn't even have life insurance, and he had 10-kids living at home. So I realized that this business was more than just about making money, and that's when it went from my head to my heart."

It went from head to heart. That's a common expression in WFG. People seem to sign on for financial independence, but if they stick around long enough, they often experience this subtle shift in thinking. Many believe they are saving people from financial ruin. The WFG platform is a powerful tool with the potential to expand far beyond materialism.

Fradel describes the power of what WFG associates do for people:

"We help people in a way that's generational. In a way that can really impact their lives for generations to come."

This was something she thought about for her own future.

"I knew that I wanted a family, but I didn't want it to be the way I grew up. I wanted my kids to have freedom, choices, and education. Things I knew that would come with money."

Back in 2004, that was big talk for a shy little 20-year-old. But Fradel Barber is no wallflower, and she proved it with her massive success. Today she's married with two children, and they have all the things she dreamed about not so many years ago. It's a true American success story. As wonderful as it was to hear her rags-to-riches story, I had to ask her about the downside of the WFG opportunity. This is what she said:

"It's you. It's the person doing it. We're human, and sometimes human nature gets the better of us. Anything worthwhile demands discipline and persistence."

New Yorkers are known for being skeptical, so I asked her how she responds to people who claim that WFG is a pyramid scheme:

"Pyramid schemes are illegal. We are not a pyramid scheme. What we are is a hybrid of three models. The first one is the corporate structure. We have the backing of AEGON. We have our corporate headquarters for World Financial Group that has employees and a President, just like a typical corporation. The corporation serves as our backbone. That allows us as entrepreneurs to operate without some of the struggles that most entrepreneurs go through. The WFG platform allows the entrepreneur to run, so they can do what they do best."

She continued:

"The other part is the network marketing aspect. We're in the relationship business, the referral business, and we work that way so we don't have to cold call and do things that are typically done to get clients. So we're able to have a business where somehow I know you, and that makes it a much friendlier conversation. And who doesn't want to do business with someone you have a connection to?"

And the third is…

"The third aspect is the franchise, where someone can be an entrepreneur, have big responsibilities, but the core structure of their business is already formatted. They have a system that's already in place. Take any franchise out there, like McDonald's or Burger King. They have a system and it's very well noted, because sometimes they have kids running it and it's still successful. WFG is a hybrid of those three models."

Well said, I thought to myself, and so true. Never thought about running a system so solid that a teenager could succeed with it.

I hated to do it, but I had to ask Fradel about what she says to the critics who claim WFG is a cult. She had a classic reply:

"Yes, we're extremely focused on business and self-improvement, and if you find something wrong with that, this is not the cult for you!"

We both laughed, but there was much truth in what she said. If WFG is a cult, it's an awfully positive one. This company has had a transformational effect on tens of thousands of people. It's had an effect on me. The world would be a better place if it were more like the WFG culture.

I asked Fradel to give her thoughts on the somewhat controversial Financial Foundation Indexed Universal Life Insurance product, and this was her unique response:

"I compare the FFIUL to a knife. A knife can be a great tool, and it can also be deadly. I think in financial services, specifically with the FFIUL, if you use it wrong it could be terrible. There are ways of setting it up where it's underfunded, it's on the wrong type of person or it's not suitable. But that's only a small percentage. For the majority of people it's extremely suitable, and it can have tremendous value in many areas of their life. It's a powerful tool if it's used in the right way. It's a product I own personally, and my whole family owns it as well."

I was impressed with Fradel's answer. It was one of the best explanations I had heard. So I decided to push a little further and ask her about another criticism surrounding this product. I said, "Some critics claim that WFG associates push the FFIUL because it's a Transamerica product and the commission is higher than other IULs." This was her response:

"I teach my team and my clients that it's mission before commission. We sell other IUL's from Nationwide, Pacific Life, and others. The truth is that the FFIUL is one of the top IUL's in the marketplace."

Once again, I was impressed with Barber's direct approach. I guess I should have expected straight talk from a New Yorker. Another interesting fact that I discovered during my interviews with WFG leaders is that so many of them own at least one FFIUL. And like Fradel Barber, many of them purchase the policy for their kids, parents and siblings. It's hard to criticize a salesperson for promoting a product they believe in so much that they purchase it for their family. I'm not saying this makes it a perfect product, but when selling it, it does boost the associate's credibility.

Moving to the next question, I asked Fradel about the low initial commissions that WFG pays new agents compared to traditional insurance companies.

"When you're with a life insurance company, you have to sell a large percentage of products from that company. You also have quotas. WFG is a much easier transition into the industry. Another big difference is the environment. Traditional life insurance companies have a sales environment. WFG has a personal development environment. One of the things that I love about World Financial Group is that it's really a personal development program with a massive compensation package attached. It places you in an environment where you're going to grow. If you took everything away from me that I earned over the past decade; money, title, accolades; there would be one thing left that you couldn't take away, and that's my personal development. That's what I've worked on with myself, with the assistance of mentors, and reading books like yours, and just learning as much as I can. That's priceless. I don't know any other company that pours in as much, and makes sure that people are developing along with their businesses as we do here."

Oh, the passion these people have, I thought to myself. No wonder they're so good at recruiting. Their love for this opportunity is genuine. I saw it in their faces and heard it in their voices. Fradel Barber was among the most passionate.

But as in any serious endeavor, there are obstacles to overcome and emotional low points to endure. I asked her to tell me about both.

"Starting out, my biggest obstacle was being shy. I really had to work on that, and I did it with the help of my mentors. I watched everybody, including my own associates and the way they prospected. One of my associates was amazing at prospecting, so I learned from her. I learned from everyone. I was a sponge.

My second obstacle was leadership. Not just leading followers, but leading leaders. That was a big challenge for me. If you're open to being in partnership, rather than being the only winner, I think that really helps to cultivate a winning environment."

Fradel described one of her emotional low points in the business:

"I hit a plateau about two and a half to three years into the business. I was making a multiple 6-figure income. I was 23-years old and I had everything I wanted. It was kind of like, now what? I felt like I needed a challenge to take me to the next level. That was when I decided to move back to New York. WFG didn't have much going on there. That's what got me out of the plateau. I thrive on challenges, and that really got me going again."

"Another emotional low-point was when I got my first perfect recruit. They were married with 2-kids and they were both interested in the business. It was the ideal family for WFG. They came on board, became clients, introduced me to their family and friends. We were in the process of training them to become the next leaders. One day the guy called me and said they were cancelling all of their policies and were out of the business. He didn't even give me an explanation. I really felt like we were friends. I tried to analyze what I did wrong, and I finally realized that I didn't do anything wrong. Sometimes you do everything you're supposed to do, but external factors affect the business. It made me stronger for the next time."

One of my biggest takeaways from my interviews is that success to these people goes far beyond the money. I would describe it as psychic income. The leaders spend a lot of time talking about money, likely because it attracts recruits, but the deeper I dug, the more emotional benefits they revealed. I asked Fradel what's given her the greatest joy in WFG in addition to her personal development journey:

"Watching leaders develop. I don't take credit for it, but maybe just having some influence. Having some impact on helping others get to where they want to be."

Now, if you're new to WFG, you may be thinking that it sounds like a perfect business. You can make money, help people and have fun. Everyone wins, right? Well, the truth is that most people don't win. They quit. So I asked Fradel if WFG is so good, why do most people drop out? Here's what she said:

"It's our society. We want instant gratification. It's not a job. Here, you have to give before you get. This is an entrepreneurial business. People have an employee mentality. People think they know better and want to do it their way."

I have to agree with Fradel's assessment. I've seen the same thing in my own industry. Everyone wants to be successful, yet few are willing to pay the price. The people who fault WFG for its high attrition rate fail to account for human nature.

I wanted to wrap up the interview on a positive note, so I concluded with a few final questions. I asked her if she had to start over again, what would she do differently?

"I would do more for longer. There were levels where I'd reach a certain point of success and slow down. I think concentrated efforts in a short period of time are much more effective than the same amount of effort stretched over a long period of time."

I asked Fradel if she had any advice to offer someone who was on the fence about whether or not to join WFG:

"Go back to that first gut feeling. Not the one you had once you thought about it, or the one you had after you talked to someone. But the feeling you had in your heart when you heard about this opportunity. Go back to that feeling and go with that. If it was bad, don't do it. But if you felt like this was your way out, like maybe you found it or you've been found, go with that. Because that's your true feeling, and you could make a difference not only in your own life, but in the lives of others."

After Fradel and some of her team members left the Mansion following the interview, I sat down with my wife to debrief. We agreed that WFG was lucky to have a young, ambitious leader like Fradel Barber. With so much negative news about the younger generations being obsessed with video games, social media and other trivial pursuits, it's good to know that there are winners like her picking up the mantle and carrying it forward.

To see the full video interview with Fradel Barber, visit www.WFGSTARS.com.

Siebold and Fradel Barber in the ballroom of the Bona Allen Mansion

Dan Charlier

DAN CHARLIER

Dan Charlier was born in Haiti, and his mother immigrated to the United States when he was two years old. Not having the money to bring little Dan with her, she saved for seven years, then brought him from Haiti to Brooklyn, New York. Charlier attended high school in Brooklyn, and after a brief stint at State Col- lege in Long Island, he decided to join the Marines. He stayed in the Marine Corps for thirteen years but became frustrated with his ongoing financial struggles. On a chance meeting with Kristianna Mylett, he was introduced to WFG and future agency chairman Ed Mylett. Being a single father with two small boys in his care, Dan was open to a new way of life. Ed called Dan, who initially told him he wasn't interested.

Ed said:

"How can you not be interested in something you don't understand? Where are you? I'm coming over."

Forty-five minutes later, Ed showed up at Dan's door, and the rest is WFG history. Dan would go on to become one of the most successful associates in WFG, and along the way, he married Christine, one of his top associates.

I met Dan and Christine back in 2005 and found them to be among the most gracious couples in the company. Behind the scenes at WFG, Dan has always been a respected and admired leader. This respect extends beyond his success. I think it's because he's so grounded. Some people call that a personality style. I call it character.

Dan and Christine are active on social media, sharing family and personal photos that depict their movie-star lifestyle. It's done in a classy, unpretentious way. I like to kid Dan and Christine that they have catalog kids because the whole family looks like they walked out of a Ralph Lauren catalog.

When you have this level of good fortune and success, it would be easy to allow your ego to enlarge your legend. Part of being successful in WFG is selling the dream life, and social media post- ings offer a powerful platform on which to accomplish this. The challenge is that many people who see these postings are struggling financially, and without the poster exercising a level of self-discipline, excessive prosperity postings can cause the average person to feel like a loser. Dan Charlier exercises such discipline masterfully, and his dream life postings are attractive yet never over the top. Maybe it's the discipline he learned in the military, or perhaps he's sensitive to the feelings of the struggling as someone who spent the first nine years of his life in one of the poorest countries in the world. Whatever the reason, Dan and Christine do it all with class.

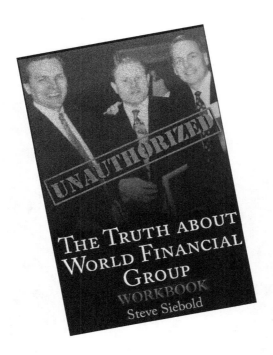

Jun Dela Cruz

JUN DELA CRUZ

Jun Dela Cruz is of Filipino descent and grew up in Southern Cali- fornia during the 1970s and 80s. After graduating with a degree in finance from California State University, Jun joined his father in the real estate business. When the market took a down- ward turn in 1993–94, he told his dad it was time to search for a different occupation. So 23-year-old Jun began his quest for a new oppor- tunity, when his godfather approached him about the company that would become World Financial Group. Jun told him that he didn't want to sell insurance, but he attended a BPM out of respect.

Jun explains what happened at that first BPM:

> *"I was impressed with the people, jumped on board immediately and started my field training. I was excited about making a differ- ence in people's lives. It was the genuine nature of the people that attracted me most."*

Jun came out of the gate like a thoroughbred, earning over $100,000 in his first year in the business. When I asked Jun how he did it, he said:

> *"They told me to do two to three appointments a week, and I started doing two to three appointments a day. I fell in love with the field right away. I fell in love with helping families. I was hooked from day one."*

During my 61-minute video interview with Jun in May of 2018, I pushed him for specifics on his success.

Here's what he said:

"My Dad was very successful, but he didn't show it. I remember a financial advisor coming to our house and talking down to him because he thought he didn't have any money. Regardless of how much or little money people have, I talk to them, not at them."

Over the years of watching Jun interact with his team, known as "Cruzader Nation" it's easy to see the love and respect they have for him. I've also dealt with him as a vendor, and he has always been extremely professional and gracious. He's a good man with a big heart.

Jun believes that one of the reasons WFG is so successful is that it's like a big family. He doesn't claim that it's a perfect family or a perfect company, but it's a family in which the members have a common goal and mission. They learn together, train together and work together. And when a member is struggling with a personal issue, the family offers its support. When Jun's father was given two months to live, Jun was devastated. His father still had things he wanted to do and accomplish. Thanks to his WFG business, Jun was able to stop working and take his dad to Europe, Canada and the Philippines to pursue alternative medical treatment. Jun's WFG family was a constant visitor to see Jun's dad, something that he believes helped keep him alive for an additional 30 months.

This experience was among the most profound of Jun Dela Cruz's life. It's another example of what makes WFG more than just a business opportunity.

If this story reads like a greeting card, I understand your skepticism. If I hadn't witnessed events like this as an outsider, I would be skeptical, too. But Jun's story paints a picture of the people whom which you're considering getting into business. Like any family, WFG is not perfect. The difference is how hard the people work to *make it perfect*.

Jun summed it up by saying:

"My best friends in this world come from WFG."

To see the full interview with Jun Dela Cruz, visit www.WFGSTARS.com.

Raja Dhaliwal

Raja Dhaliwal was born and raised in Punjab, India in a family of 10. His father was in the Indian Air Force and worked as an air traffic controller. In 2000, at 21 years of age, Dhaliwal left India for Canada in pursuit of a better life. He spoke little English but was highly motivated to become successful. He worked as a taxi driver and eventually started a residential construction business. He built homes by day and drove a cab by night. During this time, he continued searching for bigger and better opportunities. He got a commercial truck driver's license and looked into numer- ous other businesses. In 2008, while driving his taxi, he received a phone call from a stranger who was an acquaintance of a friend in Toronto. He told Raja about the opportunity and re- cruited him on the spot. Dhaliwal was a 30-year-old fireball, full of ambition and a world-class work ethic. It looked like a match made in heaven. But for the first four to five months, he was hes- itant, unsure about the business and moving slowly. The tide turned when his trainer suggested that he attend WFG's national con- vention in Las Vegas. The trainer assured Raja he could stay with him and it would be a life-changing experience. So he land- ed in Las Vegas, only to be rejected at the door. He didn't have a tick- et, the event was sold out, and the fire marshal was on hand to make sure no one else entered the hall. Dhaliwal was forced to stand outside of the arena while listening and looking through the door. He saw 16,000 people who seemed very excited about being in the room. As he watched and listened though the door to speaker after speaker, he said to himself:

"This year they won't let me in, but next year I'll be standing onstage."

The large crowd motivated him:

"I saw so many people, all believing in WFG, and I started dreaming about becoming somebody in this business. I didn't come all the way from India just to get a job. I wanted to be somebody."

And a star was born.

Raja returned to Canada and got licensed in seven days. He started building his list and learning the WFG system. And good things began to happen. That following year, 2009, Raja earned over $100,000, and by 2011, his income shot up over $250,000.

In 2018, Raja Dhaliwal hit $5 million dollar mark. The man who was forced to stand outside the convention hall in 2008 has become the talk of World Financial Group. A man who drove a cab is now a self-made millionaire.

I've spoken for Raja's teams all across the United States and Canada, and his people hold him in high regard. Recently, I was addressing his leadership team in Edmonton, and one of his top people came up to me at the break and said:

"I got into this business to make money. I'm staying in this business because of Raja. I've watched him go from cab driver to millionaire, and he's still the exact same guy."

I couldn't agree more. And that compliment is among the most important any self-made man or woman can receive. In a recent conversation with Raja, I asked him his success strategy. He said:

"Long hours and lots of appointments. You have to stay in the field if you want to be big."

I asked Raja if his humility played a role in his rise to the top, and he said:

"The more grounded you are, the more people relate to you."

One of the things I've always admired about Raja is his penchant for honesty. The MLM industry is infamous for false claims and exaggerations, but not Raja Dhaliwal. He says it like it is, and his word is gold. Knowing this, he's one of the first people I call when I want accurate numbers or facts. Recently I asked him a question that so many WFG associates and prospects ask me. It's an uncomfortable question, but it's a good one:

If WFG is such a great opportunity, why do 80% of the people quit.

Raja didn't even hesitate to answer.

He said:

"The environment in which people live kills their dreams. That's why they need to stay in our environment. That's why attending all the events is so important."

When I pushed him for more on this, he said:

"People need to stop listening to people who are quitters. They need to communicate with their leaders. You should be following your leaders instead of your leaders following you."

Raja was rolling, so I kept asking him for more advice for people pursuing the dream.

"You need to put eye blinders on. Don't be looking on the side. For the past 10-years I've done nothing but WFG. You can't lose in this business."

The last part of my interview with Raja was the most profound. I thought about it all night after our conversation. I couldn't get what he said out of my head. I asked him what kept him working so hard when many people earning millions of dollars a year would probably slow down. And jokingly, I added:

When are we going to see you driving a Ferrari and living a flashy lifestyle?

He said:

"I don't talk about Ferrari's and a lot of material things. This is not about me anymore. I'm financially solid. Now it's about helping other families so they can have the same life as me. I keep working long hours because promises have been made. I've sat down with people at their kitchen tables and made promises, and those promises must be kept."

Promises were made. The night after the interview, I kept hearing those words over and over in my head. And if you would've heard the tone in his voice, you would have felt the same. This was not some platitude he was repeating from a self-help book. This is a core belief of a man who has adopted WFG's mission of "No Family Left Behind." Only a fool would bet against a man who operates with this level of integrity.

Siebold being interviewed in Edmonton, Alberta, Canada with Field Leader Raja Dhaliwal (Pictured Far Right)

Deron Ferrell

DERON FERRELL

Deron Ferrell was born in 1957, the son of a Navy man. The family never had much money, but Deron always dreamed of becoming successful. He went on to study drama in college. One day in 1981, he received a call from his drama professor asking him to attend a Business Opportunity Meeting for A. L. Williams. The meeting was led by Jack Linder, who later would become one of the cofounders of World Financial Group. Deron explains what happened:

> *"I showed up because I heard you could make $300 a month, which meant I could afford four wheel transportation," Farrell explained. "All I had was a motorcycle, which is what I drove to the meeting. Usually you seat new prospects up front, but for some reason they stuck me in the back, behind a plant."*

Deron laughed as he recalled his auspicious start:

> *"I liked the atmosphere. I had been a convenience store clerk, roofer, sandblaster, and construction worker. Everyone was always cussing, smoking and drinking, and I went to this meeting where everyone was positive and excited. I could tell that they were glad that I was there. The crusade, the cause and the atmosphere really impressed me from the minute I walked in the door. And when Jack Linder said you could make a $100,000 a year, and I was sold! I went home that night and couldn't sleep because I was so excited. That's one of the questions I ask prospects the day after the meeting, 'how did you sleep?' If they say, 'like a baby', I'm not sure they're a good fit."*

Deron's analysis of a prospects excitement is shared by many of the leaders. If the timing is right and the prospect is ready, the opportunity offers them a new level of hope.

Deron continues telling his story:

> *"When I got involved, I didn't even have a checking account. I was renting an apartment with two other guys, and the rent was $205 a month. We were always late with the rent. I was a financial disaster! So I'm supposed to show up at your house on a motorcycle, take my helmet off and ask you to trust me with your financial future?"*

Sounds like a long shot, right? But that's exactly what Ferrell did, and while he realized only modest success, he was earning a living.

> *"I started reading self-improvement books and I tried to keep the right attitude, but I never made more than $40,000 in a year for the first 10-years."*

Deron plays it down, but during the 1980s, the median average income in the United States was around $24,000. So for a 28-year-old college dropout, he wasn't doing badly.

Still, Ferrell had expected more, and started wondering whether this opportunity was really for him. And then, A.L. Williams was acquired by Citigroup and became Primerica. Ferrell figured he had a better opportunity by defecting to the newly formed WMA, which later became WFG. And that's when his business finally took off. This is what he told me during our interview:

> *"I made $100,000 my first year with the new company. I qualified for my first trip to Hawaii after six weeks after trying for the past 10-years, and I've gone every year since."*

I asked Deron why people should choose WFG over other opportunities, and he said:

"Financial services is the largest and most profitable industry in the world. Most of us that have made it in WFG went from rags to riches. If you don't make money in WFG, it's as if we locked you up in a grocery store, came back and found you dead on the floor with a note that said; 'nobody trained me how to eat."

Only a good Texan would make such an analogy.

Deron continued:

"This is in industry, that if you do what you need to do, you're going to make a lot of money."

It's obvious that Deron believes in the opportunity, but playing Devil's advocate, I asked him about some of the downsides and the most common criticisms:

"The downside to WFG is that no one is going to do it for you. A lot of people will help, but you have to do the work. And there's no guarantee that you will make it."

Next, I asked him how he responds to people that call WFG a scam:

"We're a marketing company that represents household name companies. We help them take their products to the masses. Sometimes people think it's a scam based on the words we say. Words are the tools we use, and there are good words and nasty words. New people don't always know the best words to describe the opportunity."

I felt as though I was throwing water on the Deron's fire, but I continued with this line of questioning. I asked him what he says to people who claim that WFG is a pyramid scheme:

91

"Pyramids are illegal. Every state has an insurance department. Do you think that the giant corporations we represent would be involved in a pyramid scheme? Don't you think companies like AEGON, Pacific Life and Nationwide did some research on us? We're a highly regulated industry."

One of the criticisms people have of WFG is its low initial commission sales structure for new agents, so I asked Deron to address this:

"First of all, who wants to sell life insurance? I mean, throw up, right?

"When I was a little kid I played Army man, Astronaut, Fire man... but I never grabbed my Dad's briefcase and played insurance man! My point is that you can get a higher contract somewhere else, but ours is a multiplier. In WFG, I'm able to share the opportunity and earn a percentage of my broker's team. I have over a 100 brokers in my organization. Here, you can duplicate yourself."

Ferrell makes a key point. The traditional agent may score a higher sales contract, but it's hard to match the income potential of overriding a team of thousands of agents in your organization. It's a nonlinear commission structure in an industry that has employed a linear compensation structure for over a century.

I asked Deron to share some of his emotional low-points in the business:

"It's tough when you train people, travel with them, and get close, and then they quit. Sometimes people lose the vision and leave. They don't give it enough time. six of my $100,000 earners, with whom I started an office, cleaned out the office one night and left me with it. That was one of the toughest things I have ever experienced in the business."

To end on a more positive note, I asked Deron what had been his greatest joy in the business:

"Seeing people succeed. Seeing them get their $100,000 ring. I've had people come from nothing and make it. We have more than 50 people that have gotten their $100,000 ring. It's a great feeling that never goes away."

When I asked him to tell me his favorite rags to riches story in WFG, he laughed and said:

"Me! I was probably the worst recruit in the history of the business. I struggled for so long. But I was willing to change. I tell people all the time, don't give up on your dreams."

In conclusion to our interview, I asked Deron what advice he would offer someone considering WFG:

"Do the research. Put us to the test. Research the companies we represent. And if you really want to make a change and separate yourself from the crowd, stop doing what the crowd does. Study successful people in WFG. Find out their stories. Whatever background you have, there's someone like you who has made it."

After Deron left the Bona Allen Mansion, where we videotaped the interview, I sat down with the video crew and asked them what they thought about him. I did this because I was struck by how humble, believable and relatable Deron was. I've known him for a while, so it's not like I expected anything less, but I was struck by his sincerity and excitement about a business he's been involved in for 37 years! The vote among the crew was instant and unanimous: we all agreed that the people in Ferrell's organi- zation were among the luckiest in all WFG. Flash is fun and money is motivating, but nothing is more powerful than a sincere leader who speaks and operates from the heart.

To see the full video interview with Deron Ferrell, visit www.WFGSTARS.com.

Siebold interviewing Deron Ferrell in the studio at the Bona Allen Mansion

Chris Felton

Chris Felton was living what many might call the American Dream. It was 1999, and he was living in Denver, Colorado. He was a young, talented CPA on track to becoming a partner at the most prestigious commercial accounting firm in the world. He spent his days in corporate boardrooms teaching Fortune 500 chief financial officers how to manage their money. As perfect as Felton's life looked on the outside, all was not well within. After spending seven years with Arthur Andersen, he was looking for a change. Felton explains:

> *"I wanted to become an entrepreneur, but the search was extremely frustrating. You needed lots of capital and there was no mentoring. Not to mention that 80% of small businesses fail."*

One day he bumped into some colleagues at Arthur Andersen, Trevor Jensen and Brian Loiseau. The men looked exhausted and said they had just worked 40 straight hours. Trevor mentioned that his brother Eric was making $250,000 a year and playing golf on Fridays:

> *"Is he selling drugs," asked Felton. "I don't know, but he's coming to town in two weeks," Jensen replied.*

Two weeks later, Eric Jensen presented the WFG opportunity to the young CPAs. Jensen said they could test-drive the opportunity part time. Felton describes the scene:

> *"Eric talked about recurring income. I was blown away. I said, 'wow, how does that work?' That's what got me."*

He continues:

> *"I fell in love with the dream and vision, and I knew that I had to develop on a personal level if I wanted it to happen."*

Among the things Felton appreciated most about the opportunity were the objective promotion standards. Unlike corporate Amer- ica, where ascending the ranks is often more about politics than performance, WFG offered him the opportunity to write his own ticket. Felton explains:

> *"I asked Eric Jensen, how do I become you? He pulled out a piece of paper and showed me exactly what I needed to do. I was like 'hot damn, man!' This is it!"*

The new business was exactly for what the young CPA had been searching for. In addition to the opportunity, Felton loved the compensation structure.

> *"Your compensation is all based on raising people up. You get compensated for developing people."*

His first year was less than stellar. He earned $8,000. But once he went full time, things began to turn his way. I asked him when he knew WFG was going to be his future:

> *"When I hit $250,000 I knew I was going to do this for the rest of my life."*

Nineteen years later, Felton is an executive vice chairman in the company, along with his former Arthur Andersen colleagues.

Chris Felton is one of my favorite people. He's a successful, down-to-earth, no-nonsense businessman. He's no flash and all substance, just what you'd expect from a former protégé at a world-class accounting firm. One of the things I appreciate most about Chris is his rock-solid integrity. You can take his word to the bank. That's why he was the first field leader I invited to be interviewed at the Mansion. It's been my experience that accountants at his level rely on dead-level accuracy while avoiding hyperbole and exaggeration. He didn't disappoint, and his answers set the bar for all the subsequent interviews.

I asked Chris about his secret to success in WFG:

"Self-development and growth. One of the mistakes people make is they think the person they currently are is going to get them to their goals and dreams. They want the outside world to change while they insist on remaining the same. What I can control is my personal development. Having a morning routine that gets my mind straight, and helps me grow and develop is key. People eat every day, shower every day, but they often don't work on their mind. This combined with persistence is the secret. Most people spend significant time trying to figure out if WFG is for them or not. They should just persist until it works."

With Felton's financial pedigree, he had lots of options beyond Arthur Andersen. Many of these high-level accountants go on to become CFOs of mid- to large-size companies, eventually parachuting out with seven-figure packages. I asked him why he chose WFG:

"I looked at several different opportunities and they were the same as my job, trading time for money with no leverage. The mission didn't speak to me. The ability to teach an overlooked market how to make money work in their lives appealed to me. For generations, my family struggled with money. To combine purpose with leverage, and to be able to teach clients and agents how to become financially free, is incredible. It's the best opportunity in American business. The market is enormous and no other firm has figured this out."

When Chris said this in the interview, I thought about the magni- tude of his statement. If it came from a guy stocking shelves at a hardware store, it might be overlooked. But Felton could be over- seeing the financials of a billion-dollar corporation, yet instead he's singing the praises of a multilevel marketing company whose core market is middle- and lower-income families. His credibility alone is reason enough to consider this opportunity.

I asked Chris about the initial obstacles he faced in the early days of building his business:

> *"The guy who recruited me to Arthur Andersen shot me down about WFG. I used it as fuel. Proving people wrong was my compelling juice to move forward."*

Felton, like many accountants, is an introvert. We heard this from other leaders as well. In addition to Felton, Rich Thawley and Fradel Barber described the challenge of breaking out of their shell to build their business. These leaders prove that with enough gumption, any personality style can be successful.

I asked Felton about the downside of WFG:

> *"The downside, if you want to call it one, is people have to take 100% responsibility for their success or failure. This business shines a halogen light on your weaknesses, and where you need to improve. It gives you the necessary feedback to win in life. Some people quit as they cannot handle it and they blame the opportunity for their lack of success versus taking 100% responsibility. Another downside is you have to pay the price to win. Most don't want to even though they could."*

I asked Chris about some of the biggest obstacles he faced along the way:

"My approval addiction. A friend once told me that the biggest check I will ever write in my life is my need for approval. It causes you to hesitate, not to ask for the sale or referrals. Becoming aware of this and recognizing when it runs me has been challenging but worth the time and effort. Getting out of my own way is the biggest obstacle."

While we were talking about the challenges, I asked him to describe his low point in the business:

"My lowest point was in 2008. We were in the great recession, my life was a mess personally and financially, and business was slow. However, it was the challenge I needed to recognize the changes I needed to make. I sought out coaching and increased my personal development. Specifically, in the areas of money mentality, selling, goal setting and planning. We transformed and experienced amazing success. Event + Response = Outcome. I didn't like the event but the response was the right one whereby I had to take 100% responsibility and change the outcome. I grew as a result and I am now able to coach others through their challenges. It was a blessing."

It was a blessing? This is how successful people psychologically reframe their past experiences to serve their future interests.

I asked Chris what he would do differently if he had to start over:

"I would embrace the recruiting and building model quicker. I started more as a financial advisor than a builder. It took me awhile to figure out the most powerful piece of our business, and that's the ability to recruit and build leaders. It's also the most rewarding, both emotionally and financially. I would have enjoyed the process more. I tell people to embrace and enjoy the business even when they're going through challenges. Pain, suffering and being overwhelmed are choices. You can 'choose out' of these states of being."

As a vendor to the leaders, I've always thought WFG was one of the most misunderstood opportunities I've ever encountered.

I asked Chris what the most misunderstood aspects are, and he said:

> *"Most people misunderstand the effort it takes to get liftoff in your business, and they quit too early. It gets easier the longer you do it. They also underestimate the changes they have to make to their belief systems. They're too casual about this."*

That makes sense. Most of us have been raised with limiting beliefs about money. This holds so many of us back. The leaders train about this regularly, which is one of the things that makes the opportunity unique. I asked Chris to describe some of the other facets of WFG that makes it special:

> *"The ability to build a career in the largest industry in the world on a part-time basis. That's amazing. If it weren't for the part-time opportunity, I would not have started in the industry. The leadership and mentoring is unsurpassed. I wanted a company where I could never out grow the leadership team. WFG is that company. All of this combined with the best compensation model I have ever seen, with the ability to earn income in a myriad of ways and experience true recurring income."*

Again, dear reader, consider the source of this commentary. It's coming from a man so gifted with numbers he passed the CPA exam on the first attempt. That's how a kid right out of college gets picked by a company like Arthur Andersen. It's the equivalent of a college football player becoming a first-round draft pick.

I was getting excited listening to Chris detail the unique aspects of the opportunity, so I thought I would follow up by asking him about WFG's unique culture:

"The culture is our strength. Traditional firms in our industry want fancy degrees and backgrounds, and that is the opposite of our focus. We look for people with heart, desire, and those wanting a better life. They are construction workers, social workers, flight attendants and CPA's. People from all walks of life and nationalities. It's professional yet high energy. There is nothing like it anywhere, and it's a significant reason for our amazing growth."

Felton's not exaggerating. As I've stated earlier in the book, WFG's culture is its secret sauce. It's so special that I often wonder where people go when they quit WFG. How does one walk away from the most loving, uplifting environment imaginable? I'm not even in WFG, but I've been so struck by its culture that I wrote this book—unsolicited, I might add. That's how right Chris Felton is. Imagine the impact entering this world might have on the way you think. The possibilities are staggering.

As much as I hated to ruin the mood, I felt compelled to ask Felton to address the WFG critics:

"The critics are mostly those that gave WFG a shot and quit. Instead of taking100% responsibility for their failure, they blame the company. It's always someone else's fault. I want to know the source of their experience. If you know the company and the leadership like I do, there is only positive intention and a heart to help people. It's one of the many reasons this has been my only professional stop in the industry in 18-years. Most have been to three or more firms in that time. I always look to results versus stories from critical people."

On a more positive note, I asked Chris about his greatest joy in the business, followed by his favorite client story:

"My great joy has been watching the difference the business has made in other peoples lives, for both clients and agents. I once asked my teammates how this business had changed their lives. Marriages had been strengthened, they were teaching their kids the laws of success, and they were happier. Their health and spiritual lives improved, and financially they were better off. That's when I developed the belief that everyone's life becomes better if they just don't quit. I've collected a lot of evidence on this, and making a difference in peoples lives offers significant fulfillment."

"My favorite client story was in 2003. I was referred to a lady that wanted to retire in March of 2012. She was a CPA, CMA, and Corporate Auditor. She was very smart, however, she misunderstood one important fact about money. When emotion goes up, intelligence goes down. It did not matter how smart she was; she made bad emotional decisions with her money. She needed help. We put a plan together, helped her avoid the market meltdown of 2008, worked on her money mentality as well as the how to's. She retired in March 2012, and we ensured that she would never run out of money. She is happy and grateful that she met us. When she takes one of her three cruises a year, she always emails me about her trip and all the cool activities she's doing. She is grateful for the peace of mind around money and how we made a significant difference in her life."

What a great story. As Chris was telling it, I wondered how many people have the opportunity to experience that level of job satisfaction. As we were moving toward the end of the interview, I asked Chris what advice he would offer to a new associate or someone considering the opportunity:

"Be Coachable. We have an amazing business model and the structure incentivizes us to give good advice. As most people are unaware of the laws of success, sometimes the instruction does not line up with their existing beliefs, so they become selectively coachable, meaning they only follow advice on things that align with their beliefs. This slows them down and hinders their success. If they knew how to build a great business and be financially free, they would already be living the results. Be coachable and trust the process."

In closing, I asked Chris is there was anything else he wanted to share:

"People invest millions in franchises and business models that are not as explosive as WFG. My thought was I would invest very little money, learn more about money than I ever had, and make that investment back in a big way. People over analyze and wait for the timing to be perfect. My timing was not good. I was working 80-hours a week as a CPA, but I just got started with baby-steps and took action every single day. Just start and get moving. Clarity happens as you take action."

As with the other leaders I interviewed, Chris Felton was transparent and full of good advice. Coming from the more conservative faction of the field force, his words were measured and his demeanor disciplined. Felton is about as straight a shooter as they come.

To see the full video interview with Chris Felton, visit www.WFGSTARS.com.

Siebold and Chris Felton in the studio at the Bona Allen Mansion

Paxton and Jill Fritsch

Paxton Fritsch was born in Winnipeg, Manitoba, Canada, in 1973. His father was a military pilot in the Royal Canadian Air Force, so the family moved around a lot during his childhood. After graduating from Carleton University in Ottawa, Ontario, with a degree in law and sociology, Paxton found work at an engineering plant in Chico, California. He dreamed of becoming a police officer and eventually spent eight years with the Edmonton Police Service. To satisfy his entrepreneurial streak, Paxton owned and operated three tanning salons while he was working the beat in Edmonton. During this time, he became friendly with a gentleman named Cameron Agnew, who owned a nightclub in town. Agnew advertised his club at Paxton's tanning salon. In December of 2005, Agnew invited him to attend a WFG Business Presentation Meeting at Real Michaud's office in Edmonton. Fritsch saw the vision immediately and signed on.

Working full-time as a police officer and part-time with his three tanning salons, Paxton earned $1500 in commissions his second month in WFG. Paxton told me recently:

"I knew I was going to do this full time,"

And in May of 2006, that's exactly what he did. He asked the Edmonton Police Service if he could take a leave of absence, and he was told that he could but that they had seen this before, and he would be back. So he took a leave of absence and coasted through the summer months. In September 2006, he was ready to get serious and start treating WFG like a business. About this time, Real Michaud was moving into his new 27,000-square-foot office in Edmonton, and Fritsch put down a $10,000 deposit to secure a private office in Real's building. Fritsch explains:

"I had no money and I was $50,000 in debt. But that next year I went from making $30,000 to $50,000 a year."

In September of 2008, Fritsch attend an event where he heard that Cameron and Corey Michaud, Real's sons, had moved to Calgary and were doing well with their own office. That gave him the idea to move to Ottawa, Ontario, to do the same. And that's what he did. Paxton explains what happened in Ottawa:

"The first eight months were terrible. We were over $100,000 in debt."

But Paxton, his wife and new baby continued to fight for their dream:

"We had a crib for the baby in the office, and we started hiring staff. We started with about 3,000 square feet. I called everyone I knew and everyone I could find. If I saw a billboard on the side of the road with a Realtor on it, I'd call him. We recruited 22 people personally that first year in Ottawa."

One of WFG's great success stories was in progress. Fritsch continues:

"I focused on growing my licensed sales force. And within four years, I had 70 licensed agents. And in 2013, that's when the fun began."

Fritsch's fun meant being promoted to the CEO level of the company, meaning he had six direct senior marketing directors. And the fun was only beginning.

"In 2015 I earned about $500,000. By 2017, I had nine Senior Marketing Directors, became an Executive Vice Chairman, and earned over $750,000."

Not bad for the military kid turned cop and tanning salon owner. Paxton's next goal is to crack a cool million. No one inside of WFG will bet against him. He's too focused to fail.

I asked him to share his secrets to success:

"I'm not delusional. I compensate for my lack of skills with my work ethic. I don't make excuses and I attend every event. I do what's right."

When I asked him about the downsides to WFG, he hesitated and said:

"You have to work. It's an incredible system, but it's a volunteer army and they can leave anytime they want. It's easy to get distracted by shiny objects, other opportunities. My number one obstacle was myself. I was fearful and doubted myself sometimes. I wasn't sure of myself."

Hard to believe coming from a man who turned a $125 investment into an incredible income. I asked him which form of marketing he preferred, the flash or the crusade. He responded:

"People will stick with the business when it's based on a relationship instead of just money. The flash doesn't attract the same quality of person. I don't like to look like I'm bragging. I'd be selling my soul."

His answer didn't surprise me. The first time I met Paxton, I got a sense of his humility and charm. I thought to myself, *This is not a flashy guy, and I'll bet you can take his word to the bank.* People trust him, and I believe that's one of the reasons they follow him. I asked Paxton if he could offer any words of advice for someone considering WFG:

> *"It's an opportunity that can change your life; the best on the planet. It might be the hardest thing you'll ever do, but it can change your entire family's future."*

Fritsch currently has 250 licensed agents. "I'm going to have 10,000 licensed agents in the next 10 years," he declares. And I wouldn't doubt it for a minute.

In a world where the good guy always wins, Paxton Fritsch would be king. Fairy tales aside, this hard-hitting executive vice chairman is facing the real world head-on and taking no prisoners. He's already won the game. Now he's just running up the score.

To see the full video interview with Paxton Fritsch, visit www.WFGSTARS.com

Siebold interviewing Paxton Fritsch in the studio at the Bona Allen Mansion

Paul and Gabie Hart

Paul Hart grew up in a lower-middle-class neighborhood of San Jose, California, alongside two sisters. In a mixed area of gang members, his dad's guidance kept him on the straight and narrow. Paul played baseball in high school and developed an ear- ly interest in fixing up classic cars. "I had to fix my own cars because that's the only way I could drive," Hart explains. His parents were born and raised in the 1930s, and he describes them as traditionalists. "I grew up with poverty-class thinking," Hart exclaims. He attended college at San Jose State University, where he studied digital media and animation. During this time, he invested in a 1969 Pontiac GTO muscle car, which he started restoring. In the middle of the project, the car was stolen and never recovered. "After that, I didn't trust anyone," Hart said. He had lost his largest asset, his beloved car, and he was feeling it. Then, suddenly, fate intervened.

Paul bumped into one of his neighbors in a nightclub. The guy was a former football player who grew up down the street. His name was Eric Olson. The two reconnected, and Olson told Hart he was in the financial services business. Olson said he'd been doing it for about 18 months. Hart says.

"I thought it sounded sexy", Hart says. "I thought I might be able to get in because I knew somebody."

Hart attended a meeting and jumped right in.

"I knew I was going to do it right away. I was very money motivated. I didn't make any money my first 6-months working full-time because I had to get licensed", Hart said. "But 9-months after I got licensed, I hit $125,000. And in my second year, I made over $200,000."

Hart claims that the foundation of his business was built in the first six months. "I recruited 10 people personally in my first month, and with my team, we recruited a total of 25 people." During our interview, Paul explained that he never wanted a boss. "I hate people telling me what to do," he said. "Once I got started, all I wanted to do was WFG. I was like a WFG gym rat."

From auto mechanic to WFG gym rat—doesn't seem like a natural transition. But then again, Paul Hart is no ordinary man. He's a human fire hydrant full of ambition waiting to be let loose, and let loose he did.

While building the business, Paul met his future wife, Gabie, who was also in WFG. He had been stuck in a plateau for more than two years when Gabie introduced him to a more system-based method of building WFG.

> "My business was personality driven, and Gabie really helped our team implement the system."

It took him five years to reach the CEO level, where he was earning around $220,000 per year. And from there, his success has grown exponentially.

That's the upside, so I asked Paul about the downside of WFG.

He said:

> "It's an emotional, reputational risk. People are so addicted to approval that they surrender their own goals. And you're the most fragile when you're not making any money."

Since Hart is part of WFG's California contingent, I felt that it was important to ask him about his philosophy on marketing and recruiting. In other words, did he use the flashy, money-oriented approach or more of the crusade? This was Paul's reply:

"I'm in the middle. You have to be a chameleon. I'm always looking at whom I'm talking to. You can't recruit people to what you like, you need to find out what they like."

Made sense, but I pushed him for a little more detail, and he obliged:

"I have a team of millennial's, and they'll kill to get those flashy things. They've never had that kind of recognition. That being said, my crusade is to teach people how to have a wealth mentality. And if you lead with the more noble stuff, it works much better. It breeds more trust."

I trusted Paul Hart from the first minute I met him at our Mental Toughness University event in San Jose a few years ago. He's affable, engaging and focused. He and Gabie are close friends with Eric and Sandra Olson, yet Paul has his own unique charm and style. If Olson is the horsepower, Hart is the finesse.

Steven Holbrook

Steven Malcomb Holbrook was born in 1981 in Calgary, Alberta, Canada, the son of a bricklayer and a secretary. At age two, he was diagnosed with Crohn's disease, an incurable, chronic inflammatory bowel disease that affects the lining of the digestive tract. At age 15, he took a job washing dishes at Earl's, a high-end family restaurant. He later graduated from the University of Alberta with a bilingual business degree.

In 1999, he sailed on the 188-foot SV Concordia across the world for 10 months with 59 other kids. The adventure was among the best of his life. After Holbrook's folks took over his grandparents' masonry business, an enterprise that employed over 200 people, they invited Steve to join the team. The multimillion-dollar company would have been a safe bet for Holbrook, but instead he decided to strike out on his own. He was offered a management position at Earl's, where he had moved up to waiting tables. The restaurant had always been a kind of refuge for Steve, who because of his small stature was bullied throughout his school days. It was another opportunity for Holbrook to travel down an easy path, and once again he refused to take it.

He was unsure of his next move. A fateful trip to the local coffee shop would change his life forever. It was there that he was invited by a stranger to attend a WFG Business Presentation Meeting. Steve got fired up about the opportunity and went full time in his fourth month. The year was 2005. He was 23 years old.

Holbrook's work ethic helped him earn over $100,000 his first year in the business, an impressive sum for a newly minted college graduate. His second year, he earned over $200,000 and established himself as an up-and-coming leader. The little guy who'd survived bullying and Crohn's disease was becoming a star in WFG. The next few years were even better, until 2009, when Steve's disease flared up and landed him in the hospital for three months. Thanks to his hard work during the previous four years, Steve earned $165,000. This further solidified his commitment to the company, and when he finally came out of the hospital, he decided to go all in with WFG. He started writing sales again, and his business has grown 25%–30% every year since. One of the milestones was crossing the $750,000 income mark. While Holbrook continues to struggle with his disease, his positive outlook and drive are a testament to his toughness. He's the guy whom other leaders point to and say, "What's your excuse?"

During our recent interview, I asked Steve for the secret to his success. He said:

> *"The mental game. I'm very habit driven. I've read a chapter of the book, 177 Mental Toughness Secrets of the World Class every day for seven straight years. I'm not the most talented, but I'm very consistent."*

He continued:

> *"We have one of the top teams in the company. We have strong leadership. Our retention is high. Most of our policies stay on the books. Our licensing ratio is 20%, and 80% of our recruits become clients."*

It's easy to see why people are attracted to Holbrook. His energy and enthusiasm are contagious. At the risk of throwing water on his fire, I asked him about the downside of WFG. He said:

> *"If you're not dissatisfied, WFG may not be for you. If you're not self-motivated and coachable, it's going to be tough to succeed. You have to know what you want or you'll have a hard time getting it off the ground."*

Seeing that Holbrook is Canadian, I wanted to get his take on using flashy versus crusade marketing to recruit people. His answer was interesting:

> "I'm crusade driven, but don't get me wrong, I want to make more money. I think that people who use flashy, money-based marketing are thinking short-term. Promoting the crusade of helping families takes longer, but I prefer it to the flash and dash. The flash and dashers are not as developed."

At the end of the interview, I asked if he had any final thoughts to share, and he responded by saying:

> "The financial services industry is broken. I meet with families every day that have no insurance. The banks answer is to issue them another credit card. The middle class is underserved, and in our model, we have an incentive to serve the middle class."

He continued:

> "For me, it's about legacy. My goal is to earn $5 million dollars per year. I want to be a kingmaker. I want to be significant in people's lives. I want to create something special. Its about coaching people to be the heroes in their own lives."

The Steve Holbrook story is inspiring. Here's a man who's been battling an incurable disease his entire life, yet he continues to fight for his dreams. I think the true secret to Steve's success is mental toughness and the unwillingness to allow an ongoing series of life-threatening health challenges to define him or control his life.

Monte Holm

Monte Holm is one of the original cofounders who pledged everything he owned when the company struck out on its own in late 1991. His success story is a true tale of rags to riches. Holm grew up poor in a large family in Utah and Idaho. His father died when he was 14, leaving the teenager lost and defiant. With a 1972 Chevy Vega and $40 in his pocket, he decided to run away from home in search of freedom. He spent the next few years working odd jobs while attending college. During this time, he was approached by a man who suggested that he try his hand at the financial services industry. Holm declined but kept in touch. One year later, he changed his mind and entered the industry. By age 25, he was a millionaire.

In 2005 he became president of World Financial Group and later CEO of US and Canadian operations.

I met Monte Holm the year he became president of World Financial Group. I had seen him speak at some of the WFG meetings, and he struck me as an honest man. At that time, the vice president of marketing for WFG was a man named Bo Gibbs. Bo and I were friends, and I asked him to introduce me to Monte. The three of us met in Monte's office at WFG, and I was deeply impressed by his graciousness and sincerity.

The reason this should tell you something about Monte Holm's character is that I was, and still am, just a vendor to the company. This meeting took place behind closed doors, and in my experience, that's where you really get to know somebody. Monte Holm was candid and kind. He immediately told me how my first book, *177 Mental Toughness Secrets of the World Class*, had impacted him and many others in the company. We spoke about the goals he had for World Financial Group as president and how we might work together in the future.

During the years of Monte Holm's reign as the corporate leader of WFG, 2005-2008, I had the opportunity to meet with him several times. He was always positive, uplifting and encouraging. He's the same man offstage as he is onstage.

Now, if you haven't met a lot of rich and powerful people, this may not mean anything to you. But I will tell you that I've spent the majority of my life interviewing, serving and socializing with the self-made rich. To say they are an interesting segment of society is an understatement. These are people who have more money than they need, and that often amplifies their character and values. They can say and do whatever they want without fear of reprisal. I've discovered that this level of freedom unveils the true essence of a person. In public, they are peaches and cream. In private, they can be mean, egomaniacal and nasty.

I didn't know the young Monte Holm when he was a construction worker or missionary or when he worked at the skating rink. I met him later in life, when he was rich and powerful. But every instinct I have developed in my 53 years on this planet tells me that he's the exact same guy now as he was then, and that, my friends, is a very big deal.

My purpose in telling you this is not to make Monte Holm out to be a hero. As I've stated, I've spent my life with the rich and powerful. The riches people acquire no longer impress me. However, the way rich people behave does, especially the manner in which they treat others, specifically the people below their economic status. And that's what impresses me most about Monte Holm. I've watched him interact with people for years, and I've witnessed his warmth and generosity. Monte Holm is an example of humility, strength and leadership, and he remains a central figure in this company.

If you're seriously considering planting your flag with WFG, you need to read *Expect to Win* by Monte Holm. This book will teach you success strategies and help you further understand the heart and mind of one of WFG's most important leaders.

I earned my fortune selling training contracts to Fortune 500 companies, and I will tell you this from personal experience: a company, no matter how large or small, is made by the people who lead it. It's not the name that counts, nor its stock price or size. It's the men and women who make the rules and lead the charge. So when you're evaluating this company, study the quality, character and behavior of its leaders. That will tell you the true story and help you decide if you resonate with who they are, not just what they offer.

Juan Jaime

JUAN JAIME

Juan Jaime was born in 1982 in Mexico, the middle child with two sisters. His parents immigrated to San Jose, California. Juan's father worked as a plumber and his mother at a restaurant. Juan played soccer in Mexico and later switched to basketball and football when he came to the United States. He received a scholarship in math to National Hispanic University, a four-year private school located in San Jose. He graduated with a degree in business administration and marketing. After graduation, Juan had a hard time landing a job and began working with his dad as a plumber. He got married to Veronica, and around this time, she was invited by a friend to take a look at WFG. She wasn't inter- ested but thought her husband would be. She was right. Juan attended the Business Presentation Meeting and thought, "Man, this could be a way out of plumbing." He describes his excitement after that first meeting:

"It was awesome! I was 23-years old. Everyone in the room was young. It felt like a team. I signed up the same night."

And a great WFG leader was born.

Not just any leader, but an immigrant from Mexico who would become only one of two Hispanics to hit the million-dollar mark in WFG.

Juan details his first few months in the business:

"I lit it on fire from day one. I started recruiting immediately. The problem was I failed the license exam 4- times before I finally passed. Not because it was hard, but because I didn't study. My fourth month in the business, I finally passed."

Can you imagine a math scholar failing a life insurance exam? The turning point came when Eric Olson called Juan into his office and asked, "When are you going to get serious about getting licensed?" Juan was still earning money in plumbing with his dad, and he didn't think the commissions he was missing were substantial. When Olson showed him the numbers, they were much larger than Jaime expected. He walked out of the office realizing he was losing thousands of dollars and decided to pass the exam immediately. And that's exactly what he did.

This early failure would drive Jaime only to work harder and build bigger. In the twelve months after getting licensed, he earned $127,000. This was an astounding amount of cash to the 24-year-old immigrant, who had never seen that kind of money in his young life. As a result, his business flattened out the second year, and his income dropped down to $100,000 and stayed there for the next six years. Jaime explains what happened:

"I got comfortable. I don't come from money. I was young, and with my wife's income added in, we were making $170,000 a year."

Associates getting comfortable is something that every leader mentioned. Some, like Juan, get comfortable at $100,000 and others at $1,000,000. The problem is the same: they stop building. They stop recruiting new people personally, and they begin resting on past efforts. Jaime fell into this trap. His wife, Veronica, eventually confronted him. "I know you're better than you're showing," she said. And Juan knew she was right. He was also feeling the weight of not living the lifestyle that he was promoting. He says.

"Sometimes we sell the dream to other people, and we're not living it," he says.

The shift came at a national convention, where Juan heard Jeff Levitan speak about thinking bigger. He explains the moment that would catapult his business into the big leagues:

> *"I told my wife to quit her job. We planned it out. We paid off $9,000 in credit card debt and saved one year of her income. It was a 12-month goal, but we were so committed that we achieved it in five months."*

Veronica quit her job and started working with her husband full time. It was the catalyst that would help skyrocket their business:

> *"In 38-months, we went from earning $100K per year to over $1 million."*

I asked Jaime what drove him to make such a massive leap:

> *"Besides the money, I wanted to be Eric's number one guy. I would take a bullet for him."*

This fierce loyalty to Eric Olson is a common theme among his highest-ranking generals. It's not just loyalty to a leader; it's a fierce connection that's unmistakable when you're among them. I would describe it as an "us against them" culture, with Olson serving as the team's fearless leader. It's not a cult, but it's certainly a cultlike culture. It's what any leader would die for, yet in corporate America, it's nearly nonexistent. Olson isn't leading his team from an ivory tower; he's arguably the hardest-working, most-bloodied man in the battle. And his comrades know it.

Today, Juan and Veronica Jaime have 650 licensed agents on their team, whom they train out of their own 10,000-square-foot office. After 13 years, at age 36, Juan Jaime is one of WFG's brightest young stars.

During our recent interview, I asked him what the downside was to WFG:

> *"We lose a lot of people early in the business. People don't stick around to understand it. You have to explain to them what they're getting into. If they knew what I know, they would never quit."*

I asked him about his marketing and recruiting strategies:

> *"I recruit people based on the mission of building a business. If they're only here for the money, it's the wrong reason. You're not going to get rich in 12-months. If you want to build a business, you're in the right place."*

One of the questions I've asked dozens of leaders in WFG is one they don't enjoy. The question is, "If WFG is such a great opportunity, why do so many people quit?" I asked Jaime the same question:

> *"90% of the people who sign an AMA quit in the first 18-months. Xuan Nguyen says that 'no one is real until they've been in for 18 months'. Some of it is the way they're recruited. Some people say "Hey, you want a job?" and WFG is not a job, it's a business opportunity. Another issue is that we can't control what people are saying, both online and off. When people are recruited the wrong way they get a bad taste of the business."*

There's no doubt that Juan is right. I've witnessed it myself. But I think he's being overly polite. I've seen thousands come and go, and here's what I've concluded: Most people are lazy. They're nice people. They sincerely want to be successful. They love the idea of helping people. But they're lazy. They want the success without the suffering. And when it fails to happen, they quit and blame a company that provides only a platform. It's sad but true, and it will never change. That's what makes leaders like Juan and Veronica Jaime so special. They dream big, talk bigger, and back up their big words with massive action. That's called integrity, and these dynamic young leaders have it in spades.

I asked Juan to share his secrets to success:

"I'm emotionally stable, and a lot of people are not. Their emotions go up and down with the business, but mine don't. I'm real, and I think I'm a good guy. I'm the same person both off stage as I am on. I'm a hard worker and I'm competitive."

Juan's right. He is a good guy. And a workhorse. I asked him about the impact that Veronica has had on his success:

"Veronica is my secret weapon. She brought a whole different environment to our organization. She keeps me in check."

I asked him if he thought that couples who work together have an advantage:

"Absolutely, but that doesn't mean single people can't win big. But as a couple, you can be unstoppable if you're both on the same page."

This is a commonly held belief in WFG, and it's backed up by some pretty strong data. The power couples in WFG are legendary. I concluded the interview by asking Juan if he could offer any advice to people who are considering WFG:

"The fact is that if you're interested enough to read this book, you should give it a try. Just do it. Follow the system and follow your leader."

Juan and Veronica Jaime rank among the top leaders in WFG, and my prediction is that their legend will grow. They're focused, successful and committed.

It turns out that millennials get a bad rap. Not all of them spend their days playing video games and job-hopping. Some, like Juan and Veronica, are breaking records and leading people to success.

Jeff Levitan

JEFF LEVITAN

Jeff Levitan was born on the south side of Chicago. His dad was a truck driver, and his mom worked as a waitress. He watched his parents struggle with money and eventually divorce. Levitan graduated from Illinois State University with a degree in finance. He dreamed of becoming a financial advisor and possibly working on Wall Street. His first job out of college was selling life insurance with Minnesota-based Federated Insurance. After completing his field training, he was assigned to his territory in Milwaukee, where he sold commercial property and casualty insurance. The daily process of cold-calling helped him develop thick skin, but after two and a half years, he was ready for a new challenge. About this time, a friend in Jeff's apartment complex approached him about a new business opportunity. The two men played volleyball and worked out in the gym together, so he agreed to take a look. Levitan explains how he felt when his friend approached him:

"It was strange and awkward, as it usually is."

But he agreed to meet with his friend's mentor, Greg Kapp.

"I wasn't happy at Federated, and I didn't like cold calling. I wasn't getting paid what I was worth. I was ambitious, hungry and frustrated with my job."

"I got excited about the opportunity right away. I could read and understand insurance policies. And I didn't have Merrill Lynch or Morgan Stanley knocking down my door. I chose WFG because they recruited me."

And with that, a giant was born. Within nine months, Levitan was pulling down $4,000–5,000 per month, a substantial sum in 1995. He decided to plant his flag, quit his job and go full time.

Today, within the gated community of WFG, Levitan is a legend. He's one of the highest money earners in the history of the company. He, his wife and his five children live on a sprawling estate on the outskirts of Atlanta that would make a movie star blush. The blue-collar kid from Chicago is living the American Dream.

I've known Jeff for close to 13 years, and I witnessed his storybook ascent to the top. He's always seemed unaffected by his success. Maybe I see him this way because he's a fellow Chicagoan. I relate to a lot of the things he says because I hear the conservative midwestern influence. For all its size and prosperity, Chicago is not a flashy town, and its people are among the most down to earth you will encounter. A good example is when Jeff invited his parents to see his new home. The first thing Jeff's dad said was, "Why do you need all of this?" This is a classic Chicago response. I had a similar experience with my dad when I showed him my first large home. My dad said, "How much are the property taxes on this palace?" followed by, "That roof is huge. Did you inspect it for leaks before you closed? It'll cost a fortune if you have to replace it."

So much for attaboys! But 25 years later, I've grown to appreciate this conservative approach. And for all his wealth and success, I see the same in Levitan. He's a local boy who made good, and I have a strong feeling that no matter how much richer he gets, he'll never change.

As much as I had learned about Jeff over the years, I asked him to come to the Bona Allen Mansion so I could ask him a series of questions, questions I knew wouldn't get past the company's compliance department.

One of the nasty things that people read about WFG on the Internet is that it's a scam. You can Google "WFG scam" and read all about it. But after 13 years of being behind the scenes, I don't recognize the company depicted by these critics. So I asked Jeff point blank, "Is WFG a scam?" As always, he was forthcoming:

"We're in a highly-regulated industry, so it's hard to run a scam.

132

We wouldn't have been in business this long if we were a scam."

I asked him another hard-hitting question:

"Is WFG a cult?"

Jeff replied:

> *"WFG is a team, not a cult. We like to have fun. We take the fun, excitement, and recognition of Network Marketing, combine it with the proven duplicable systems of franchising and add in the great products of traditional financial services. We are a combination of three great industries, but we are not a cult."*

I was on a roll, so I asked Jeff to give me the downside of WFG. Here's what he said:

> *"The downside of WFG is you have to work. You have to pass a licensing exam. Then you have to face rejection in prospecting people."*

A classic Levitan response: short, simple and straightforward. Next I asked him another uncomfortable question. I said, "What's the thing that prospects dislike most about the WFG opportunity?" And he said:

> *"Recruiting. The network marketing piece. So, tell I them right way that they don't have to recruit anyone. They can make a fantastic living just selling financial services. We have a good percentage of associates who only sell financial services."*

I responded by asking him why people join WFG if they only want to sell when they can earn higher commissions selling with a traditional financial services company. He replied by saying:

"The traditional financial services industry is very exclusive. Not everyone can play. WFG is inclusive. We're willing to give everyone a chance to make it."

How can you argue with that? I found his answer to be refreshingly fair. Levitan's claim is accurate as well. Getting hired by a traditional financial services firm is no easy task. I applied at Merrill Lynch a few years out of college, and they wouldn't even grant me an interview. While I might have been unqualified, WFG would have given me a chance.

As we continued our conversation, I asked Jeff about his marketing and recruiting philosophy, specifically as it relates to employing flashy material possessions to lure prospects. This is what he said:

"I don't believe in the strategy of fake it until you make it."

One of the financial products that WFG represents is called Finan- cial Foundation Indexed Universal Life Policy, or FFIUL. Almost all the WFG leaders I interviewed for this book claim to own at least one or more of these polices, yet there have been numerous complaints from consumers. So I asked Jeff about this product, and here's what he said:

"On financial products and services, there are lots of contradictory opinions, even from top experts. None of our products are perfect, but most of them are really good. When people criticize our products, I simply ask them if they have something better. Because if they do, maybe I'll put my money there."

One of the more staggering statistics in World Financial Group is the percentage of people who sign an AMA, yet fail to get licensed. According to my internal sources, fewer than 10% of associates ever get licensed. I've known this for years but never understood why, so I asked Jeff:

"In my opinion, the ratio of licensing is low not because the test is hard or because people don't try it. There are just a lot of people that sign up and never even take step one."

Then I asked him why some teams get half of their people licensed while others get as little as 2%. Jeff's response was:

"The teams with higher licensing percentages don't recruit as many people."

Another one of the biggest complaints with MLM companies is their high attrition and low success rates. I asked Jeff about both:

"Anytime people complain about attrition or question our success ratio, I have an answer. People don't love the answer, but it's a true answer. And the answer is that most of the people we bring on board, maybe we shouldn't. Maybe other financial companies wouldn't give them a chance. We just happen to believe in people, so we extend an opportunity to them that most people wouldn't."

Near the end of the interview, I asked Levitan what advice he would offer someone considering a career with WFG:

"What if you don't try it and it would have worked? Give it a try. If it doesn't work out, what have you lost?"

My final question was to ask Jeff what question he wished I would have asked him that I hadn't. He replied:

"You asked me a lot about the criticism of the company, but I wished you had asked me what I liked most about it."

That was by design, of course. You can read about the benefits on the company's website or in a brochure. Facts about the negative aspects of the opportunity are more difficult to come by.

That being said, I asked Jeff the question he was waiting to answer: What you do you like best about WFG? This is what he said:

> *"It's such a low cost of entry. People come here and get a financial education. I can't think of anyone, outside of the financial industry, that couldn't benefit from it."*

I concluded by asking Jeff if he had any final thoughts about the company:

> *"This company was created by good people to solve a problem, and it's working. We're not perfect, but we're working on it."*

To see the full video interview with Jeff Levitan, visit www.WFGSTARS.com.

Siebold interviewing Jeff Levitan in the studio at the Bona Allen Mansion

Tom Mathews

TOM MATHEWS

Tom Mathews is one of the cofounders and was born and raised in Cincinnati, Ohio, the son of a certified public accountant. He took an early liking to playing the trumpet in grade school and even dreamed of becoming a professional musician. He attended Xavier University in Cincinnati, graduating with a degree in accounting. In 1982, when Tom was 22 years old, he picked up a newspaper with some want ads that his dad had circled for his brother, and he saw one that read, "Overworked? Underpaid? I Need Management People Who Want to Earn \$50,000+." Tom was interested for himself, so he responded and attended a presentation. Fred Johnson explained the Rule of 72, a method of determining how long it will take an amount of money to double given a fixed annual rate of interest. Tom was upset because he had just completed his degree in accounting and he had never heard of it. He asked his dad, a CPA, who said he had never heard of it either. Tom describes how he felt during the meeting:

> "I felt this surge, that this was going to be my life's work—teaching people how money works."

Mathews's enthusiasm for a story that happened over 35 years ago was palpable and genuine. It was as if time had stood still. He continued:

> "The minute I got around this business, I just knew it was for me. We wanted to build a company that did what was right for the consumer. Not the agent or the product provider, but for the consumer."

I asked Tom how long it took him to become successful:

"It took me four to five years to really get it rolling. I was young and single, and I had no experience and a lot to learn. And if something is going to become your life's work, you learn it differently. After 10-years, during which time over 1.5 million people had joined, I was ranked among the top 50 in the company."

I asked Tom what motivated him beyond the money:

"We're righting wrongs. One wrong is people not knowing how money really works. Another potential wrong is that you might not have access to the products you need."

In 1982, 22-year-old Tom Mathews had the world at his feet. Unlike some others, he had options. I asked him why he picked this opportunity over the others:

"In WFG, we have strength of selection. We have many products. When you go to work with some companies, you can only sell their products. And in WFG there's no real overhead. For the cost of a license, you can get started and build your business. Literally, after your first sale, you have a chance to be in the black."

Tom and his wingman of over 30 years, Bill Mitchell, host webinars, Livestream video events and podcasts for their team across North America. Tom and Bill went to high school together. These guys operate like family because they are; their wives are cousins. Considering Tom's tenure in the business, I wondered how he would answer the question about what he coaches his team to lead with, the products or the opportunity. This is how he responded:

"Our flagship product is our business opportunity. We're in the business of building distribution, and that means opening outlets. In a traditional business, that means having a storefront or an office. With us, it's a new associate."

I followed up by inquiring about whether more people are interested in financial assistance or building a business. He replied:

"Some people are more into the business side and others just want to be a client. We try not to have a crystal ball."

As always, I had to ask about the downside of the WFG opportunity.

"If you're part-time, I can't think of any downside, because you're getting your bills paid by your full-time job. When I started, I was an accountant, but there was still a lot of financial knowledge I didn't have. I figured that even if I go through this training and I'm terrible at the business, I'm still going to have financial knowledge I can use for the rest of my life. Once I got the financial knowledge, I was bursting at the seams. I had to go and tell everybody. My friends would say, 'calm down!' but they were all intrigued."

With all the years of research Tom's organization has conducted in testing people's financial literacy, I wanted to know what percentage of people really understand money. He said:

"One out of three. And the financial industry is incentivized to keep it that way. The less you know, the bigger their buildings are."

Seeing that Tom was now one the patriarchs of the industry still actively building the business, I decided to ask him about the controversial Financial Foundation Indexed

Universal Life insurance policy, or FFIUL. His response showed his depth of understanding of this popular offering.

> "The cost of insurance goes up as you get older. The IUL gives the client a chance to get a market return without taking market risk, because the product has caps at the top and floors at the bottom. So you can't lose money. They also have living benefits in case you get sick along the way. You could add a long-term care rider. And don't forget the death benefit. The primary reason that you buy one of these policies is in case you don't live long enough to complete your strategy. This will help your family complete it. Your family gets a lump sum with tax advantages because death benefits are tax-free. That gives your family protection. To me, the IUL is like a Swiss Army knife type product. It doesn't do everything, but the things it can do, it does in one product. I believe it's a great product and that's why I own it. It has a lot of great features and benefits. I want to be better off if I die too soon or I live too long, and in my opinion, IUL can be a great vehicle to do a lot of things."

Another objection I asked Tom to weigh in on is that most WFG associates are not fiduciaries and are therefore only legally obligated to serve their clients under a suitability standard—in other words, to recommend products that they deem suitable for the clients' needs. Legally, the advisor does not have to serve the best interests of the consumer and can therefore recommend high-commission products in the same way any other salesperson might. An argument can be made that WFG associates are not serving high-net-worth and ultra-high-net-worth clients since many of them insist on their advisors being fiduciaries. For the more sophisticated investor, I asked Tom to address this issue:

> "Our business is based on relationships. Even if you're not a fiduciary, you should always act like one. Associates should have all their licenses. No one wants a partially licensed advisor."

Like all the leaders I interviewed, Mathews never refused to answer a question on camera. And when you're digging in during an interview, that's rare. The deeper I dug, the more Mathews and his colleagues seemed to enjoy it. It was as if they'd been starving to address their critics and share their side of the story. At this point in the interview, I felt I had hit Mathews with enough questions to quell the critics and wanted to move on to tapping into the wisdom of a WFG leader who's forgotten more about this business than most associates will ever know. So I asked him about whether his team focuses more on sales or recruiting:

"We focus on both sales and building a team. You can build a bigger business faster by building a team."

During the research for this book, one of the things I uncovered was a huge disparity in licensing ratios between the different hi- erarchies. On average, fewer than 10% of all WFG associates who sign an AMA become licensed agents. On Tom Mathews's Wealth- Wave team, it's as much as half. I asked him why his numbers were so much higher than many others:

"We've created a culture where if you don't get licensed, you can't do this. It really should be 80 to 90%."

Mathews was one of the most tenured financial service professionals that I interviewed, so I had to keep reminding myself to ask him about the old days, specifically how they compare to today's opportunity in WFG. I asked Tom if the good ole' days were better than today, and this was his response:

"It's so much easier to build the business today because of technology. We use video presentations so people don't feel like they're being sold. You can build a bigger business faster. People can now do in months what took us years because of the technology. The biggest earner in our company probably hasn't joined us yet because of technology."

The whole video crew was getting excited listening to Mathews talk about the future of the company, so like any respectable interviewer, I felt compelled to throw water on the fire. After all, I told myself, I'm looking out for the little guy who's considering coming on board with this company, not the millionaire associate. I said:

"If WFG is such a great opportunity, why do so many people quit."

I honestly thought Tom would look disappointed when I asked the question, but he didn't even blink. He said:

"It's human nature. Like people who join health clubs and never use them, or people that go on diets or say they're going to quit smoking."

I found it hard to argue with his answer. Then I started thinking about my diet. I realized at that moment that I was never going to become the next Mike Wallace, at least not by interviewing Tom Mathews and his WFG comrades. The smoking gun I was searching for didn't exist. Oh sure, WFG has its share of problems, just like any organization. Mother Teresa would have had problems if she put 70,000 licensed agents on the streets. But corruption or cover-ups? I couldn't find any. All I found, Tom Mathews included, was a group of sincere, excited entrepreneurs looking to help people protect their families, help them prosper, and become financially independent in the process.

Isn't that what American Free Enterprise is all about?

Isn't that the foundation of capitalism?

But I digress. Back to Tom Mathews. I told Tom that this book was being written to help the new person considering WFG make a decision whether or not to sign on, and I asked if he could offer any advice to that individual. Here's what he said:

"Don't just trust what somebody says. Do your homework. Use your eyes, your heart and your instincts. Meet the person who invited you and look at their office. Look at the way they dress. Listen to the things they say and how you feel about it. Anything you can check out, check out and you'll know very quickly. The nobility of what we're doing speaks for itself. If it works out, you like it and do well, I'm not sure there's anywhere else where you could be as successful as you could be here."

Reflecting on a 36-year career that's still going strong, Tom shared his thoughts:

"What I'm most proud of is what we've done for families that have trusted us with their money, and what we've done for associates that have trusted us with their life's work. As long as we've delivered to those two groups of people, my career is a success."

With Mathews now crowding 60 years of age, I asked him where his work goes from here:

"I think we have a legitimate chance to change financial literacy in North America. That's my ultimate business goal."

A noble goal, I thought. But then I started thinking back to the days when I was 25 years old. I was young and hungry, and I wanted to be rich. So with that reader of this book in the back of my mind, I asked Tom this question: If you were to start over today, at age 22, with all the new products, systems and technologies, how long would it take you to earn a million dollars a year in WFG?" He didn't answer right away. Remember that this guy has a degree in accounting. He's conservative, cautious and careful not to engage in hyperbole. He's a man who measures his words and thinks before he speaks, which is exactly why I asked him this question. And then he said:

"Two to three years."

I was taken aback. I've been in business for almost as long as Tom Mathews, and by any standard of measurement, that's a lot of money in a short period of time. If true, I thought to myself, any- one with even a moderate pinch of ambition should be eyeing this opportunity. I fell into a soft haze as I sat onstage facing Tom. When I should have been asking him the next question, I found myself imagining the opportunity Mathews's people have being mentored by him and the other leaders at Wealth-Wave (Mathews's organization within WFG), all for the cost of licensing. I wondered if these people understood the magnitude of this mentorship and how much I hoped that they would take advantage of it. I found myself wanting to turn back the clock 30 years and slip into their shoes. I laughed at the prospect and how irritated Mathews might have become as I hid in his back pocket, carried his bags and mowed his lawn in order to absorb every morsel of wisdom he uttered as I rose through the ranks to becoming a WFG millionaire. Then I shook myself back to reality, with Tom waiting patiently for me to ask my next question. I asked him what he believed was the secret of his success.

"I made it because I practiced. I learned that when I was a musician. I was first chair in every band I ever played in. I practiced and worked harder than everyone else. So, when it came time to play, I nailed it and they didn't. I took the same mindset into this business. I haven't seen too many people work really hard like that in WFG and not make it."

To conclude the interview, I asked him if there was anything else he wanted to say about WFG, to which he replied:

"Our leaders are the most incredible people I've ever met. They're so serious and committed to what we do. They believe at their core level that this is what they want to do for the rest of their lives."

I could have asked Tom questions for the next 24 hours, and in fact, I did contact him a few times after this interview for more information. I had always been a Tom Mathews fan, and not surprisingly, I walked away from the interview an even bigger fan. As my late business partner, Bill Gove, used to say, "He's one of the good guys."

To see the full video interview with Tom Mathews, visit www.WFGSTARS.com.

Jay Maymi

Jay Maymi was born and bred in Spanish Harlem, a neighbor-hood in Upper Manhattan, New York City. His father worked at a dry cleaner and as an elevator operator, and money was tight. In 1992, at 21 years old, young Jay got his start in the financial services industry with Primerica. His entrepreneurial mindset and hardworking habits were a perfect match for the industry. Five years into this new venture, Maymi was earning more mon- ey than he'd ever made in his life. But in 1999, he decided to leave Primerica and join WFG. A meeting with WFG legend Bill Mitchell sealed the deal. During our interview, Jay explained:

"The person who attracts you to the opportunity should be the reason you join. I joined because of Bill Mitchell."

Changing companies meant that Jay had to start over, but with seven years of experience under his belt, he was able to earn over $100,000 in his first 18 months. Jay's income would continue to rise, but he felt that something was missing. At a national convention in Las Vegas, a chance meeting with Ed Mylett gave him the answer. Ed asked Jay if he was following the WFG system, and Jay realized he was skipping steps and improvising. Jay explains:

"I wasn't coachable. I had blueprints that needed to be deleted. It took me nine months of struggling to realize that I needed to change."

Maymi took Mylett's advice and started following the system, and his business went into hypergrowth. When I interviewed him in April of 2018 at the Bona Allen Mansion, he was excited about his next big promotion in WFG. I asked him about some of the objections that arise from people considering the opportunity.

Here's a short transcript of our conversation:

— **Steve:** What do you say to people that call WFG a cult?

— **Jay:** If loving on people, getting excited for them, being positive and having a certain level of ambition is a cult, then I'm in.

— **Steve:** But you see where they're coming from, right? People dressing in their team colors, yelling out team slogans and passionately following the same ideology.

— **Jay:** Sure, but how is that any different than sports fans following their teams? Or people at political rallies chanting their favorite candidates names? No one says that these groups are cults.

— **Steve:** Good point. Ok, lets talk about another criticism people lob at WFG: The hard sell. There have been reports of people being pressured to sign up. How do you address that?

— **Jay:** We have over 70,000 licensed associates, so I'm sure there are some people who use a hard sell approach. I don't believe in the hard sell style. If you have to drag them to the table to sign up you'll have to drag them to everything else.

— **Steve:** What's your most meaningful client story?

— **Jay:** I had a client that wanted to cancel his policy, but luckily I talked him out of it. 4-months later his wife walks into my office and tells me he passed away. She said she had three small children and wondered if the policy was still active. The sense of relief she had when I told her it was, is hard to explain. It's not something you can explain in a WFG brochure.

— **Steve:** What advice would you offer to people reading this who might be sitting on the fence regarding this opportunity?

— **Jay:** I encourage them to give it a try. What have you got to lose? I suggest that they ask themselves this question: if this opportunity works, how will it change your life? Hang on to that little voice that tells you to give it a shot.

— **Steve:** Any advice for new associates just getting started?

— **Jay:** Yes. Don't buy into the flukes. The people that get in and go straight to the top are flukes. Keep things in perspective. Don't have unrealistic expectations. You may have to go through lots of trials and tribulations before you make it.

Jay Maymi is one of my favorite examples of a star associate that came from nothing and worked his way up the ladder, kicking and scratching his way to success. That's the American story. It's the Canadian story. It's the WFG story.

To see the full video interview with Jay Maymi, visit www.WFGSTARS.com.

Cameron Michaud

CAMERON MICHAUD

Cameron Myles Michaud was born on June 23, 1973, in St. Paul, Alberta, Canada. He describes it as a town where everyone wants to play pro hockey. He graduated with a degree in civil engineering from the University of Alberta, and then he moved to Calgary. He was making a good living working for Cana Construction, about $60,000 a year. Cameron worked on the Hyatt Regency Hotel and the expansion of the Telus Convention Center. Michaud explains:

"I was in the honeymoon phase of engineering, explains Michaud. But I couldn't see myself being an engineer for 30-years."

One day his father, Real, invited him to attend a WFG Business Presentation Meeting. Cameron was intrigued because his dad seemed to have a new energy and passion. The younger Michaud saw the vision immediately. He describes his response to the presentation:

"I thought; this is a chance to build the life I wanted."

But it wouldn't be so easy. Cameron had struggled with a speech impediment, and as a result, he had avoided public speaking for 25 years. To make matters worse, he didn't know anyone in Calgary. Michaud explains:

"I called my dad and asked him if this was something I could do. He said, 'Well, I guess.' He was really tentative. He knew I'd have to quit my job, not to mention my speech impediment. And I had just gotten married. But I was sick and tired of running from my stuttering. I knew I had more in me."

He continued:

> *"If I struggled through it, I gave my family a chance. If I didn't, I had no chance."*

And as any true Canadian will tell you, never underestimate a hockey player, especially if the back of his jersey says Michaud:

> *"I decided that my goals were bigger than my fears. Plus my wife thought I could do it."*

She was right.

Michaud hit the WFG ice like a champion and earned almost $50,000 his first year in the business. And that was just the beginning. In his second year, Michaud raked in $160,000, followed by $238,000 in year three. By his fifth year, he was earning over a half-million dollars. Michaud explains what drove him:

> *"Every dollar I was making was another family being helped."*

It looked as though there was no end to the boy wonder's potential. Then something happened. Michaud explains:

> *"I got stuck at $500,000", explains Michaud, "I stopped doing the things that got me to $500,000."*

Now, I can guess what you're thinking: getting stuck at earning $500,000—what a terrible tragedy! I mean, this was truly a first-world problem. That being said, getting stuck at a specific income level is a common occurrence in WFG, and its often the result of the associate getting too comfortable. And while half a million dollars is a lot of money, the mindset that creates stagnation is one to avoid at any income level.

As you'd expect, Michaud fought back. He describes what happened:

> *"I had to rebuild my fire. I had to add emotion. I didn't change what I did in the business. I just had to have some bigger reasons to fight in the business."*

He continued:

> *"I started adding some goals. A nicer car, vacation home, etc."*

Now, if this gives you the impression that his motivation was all about money, then you don't know Cameron Michaud. When I asked him about his emotional drivers, he said:

> *"If it's about helping families, you'll always do the business. It's not about hitting a number; it's about helping people. I have teammates who are struggling. I want to have significance in their lives."*

He continued:

> *"My Dad hasn't ever forgotten the little guy. Because he once was the little guy."*

Michaud would eventually break through his own barrier and go on to earn millions in WFG. I asked him what impact his junior hockey experience had on him:

"Coach-ability is a big one. I go all-in. I sink my teeth in."

I asked him about the downside of the business:

"The time and effort that it takes. People overestimate what they can do in a short period of time. You constantly have a mirror being put in front of you."

He continued:

"People don't know what they want. You have to have a picture of what the end will be."

As we were wrapping up the interview, I asked Cameron what advice he would offer to someone considering WFG:

"Find out what's missing in your life. Ask yourself if your life could be better in the next 5-years, what would that look like? Then create a picture of what you want and start putting the pieces of the puzzle together. The beginning is always the hardest, and the final pieces are the fastest."

He continued:

"Everything has a blueprint, and it has to be clear."

I asked him if he had any advice for associates that may be struggling to make it:

"In this business, everything is numbers. It's predictable."

Spoken like a true engineer.

Corey Michaud

Corey Michaud is the son of Real Michaud and the brother of Cameron. Growing up in Edmonton, Alberta, Canada, the younger Michaud was a standout hockey player and dreamed of playing in the pros. He made it to Canada's famous Capital Junior Hockey League, the feeder system to the minor pro league. Corey was earning $300–$400 a month and eventually realized it was time to go back to school. He attended Red Deer College, where he continued to play hockey, and he later studied finance at Northern Alberta Institute of Technology. After college, Michaud spent four years working at one of Canada's largest banks, where he served in a variety of roles, including processing agricultural loans.

During this time, Corey's father, Real, joined WFG and began making headway in the business. Two years later, Corey's brother, Cameron, joined his father in WFG, and two years after that, Corey quit his job at the bank and went full time with WFG. He was 25 years old and had $30,000 in savings to carry him through the launch of his WFG business. Corey explains:

"My Dad was making about $200,000 a year with WFG when I started, but I struggled for the first 10-months in the business. I didn't apply myself and I wasn't coachable. It was tough taking direction and being accountable to my Dad. And I respect my Dad so much. It was my fault."

Maybe it was his many years of training on the ice or possibly the Michaud family work ethic that kicked in. Whatever the reason, Corey Michaud turned his WFG business around and eventually became a household name in the company. Corey readily admits it wasn't easy. Not all his friends were supportive, which can be a formidable obstacle for someone in his mid-twenties. Michaud explains:

*"I thought about quitting a lot, but it wasn't because of the company",
Michaud explains. "I always trusted the company, but I struggled with
myself."*

This is common among WFG's top leaders. They are very transparent when it comes to describing their battle to the top. This
gives aspiring WFG stars hope. They realize that big earners like
Corey Michaud are not machines but fallible human beings wres-
tling with similar self-doubt.

Now a 15-year veteran of the business, 40-year-old Corey is a
force to be reckoned with. I asked him about his secret to success.
He claims::

> *"Consistency", claims Michaud. "I've never been the superstar,
> but I've been consistent. And being able to compartmentalize my
> emotions."*

Corey's answers take you inside the mind of a great athlete
turned businessman, a star who doesn't see himself as a star. He's
been trained to compare his performance to the best in the world,
not the average person. It's a level of training few people receive
and even fewer understand. The same applies to his comments
regarding compartmentalization, which every finely tuned athlete learns to master. Last but not least is his humility, which I
would attribute to fine parenting. I can't imagine the son of Real
Michaud as anything but humble. It's the Michaud way:

> *"I grew up in a house where we were taught to treat people as we
> wanted to be treated. And to always be fair with people. As my
> Dad's business grew big, I watched him. No matter how big he got,
> he took calls from everyone, including brand new people."*

I asked Corey about the biggest obstacles he faced as his business
grew:

"When you recruit people into the business, you get deep with them. You build this dream together, and then they quit. That's one of the hardest things."

I've heard this comment from WFG leaders over the past 13 years. They train these people. They spend time with them. They travel together, and then suddenly, some of them drop out of sight, never to be heard from again. This seems to be one of the heartbreaking aspects of the opportunity and, if you decide to pursue it, something for which you should be prepared. I've never heard a leader express it this way, but I think they often fall in love with their people, especially the ones who share their dream. This is certainly one of the downsides of the opportunity. I asked Corey about some other downsides. He explained:

"So few people today are willing to work beyond the status quo. People want something for nothing", he explained. And once someone reaches $100,000 per year, it's too easy to do nothing. It's too easy to not be accountable."

Being a Canadian in a US-based company presents an interesting challenge. I have spoken for WFG teams, including Corey's, throughout Canada and the US, and I have seen that the culture is very different. Canadians tend to be more conservative in their approach and more polite in their discourse. So I asked Corey about these differences and whether or not he agreed with the flashy approach some of the American leaders employ in their marketing and recruiting efforts. Says the former hockey star:

"I'm not a flashy guy", said the former hockey star. "I drive a Ford truck. People don't care what kind of car you drive or home you live in. They care about how you make them feel. Part of the way you recruit is based on what you want people to say about you. It's about your reputation. Treat people the way you want to be treated. I learned this from my Dad. They hold him in high regard."

In the interest of full disclosure, I will admit to being slightly biased about the Michaud family before I conducted this interview. I've watched this family behind the scenes with one another and with their teams. I've spoken to thousands of their people over the years, so I approached this interview with a warm feeling toward the younger Michaud. But I was moved after my extensive interview with Corey. The combination of his transparency, humility and business/life philosophy left me thinking about how lucky his team is to have him as a leader. And the last thought I had after I interviewed him was that Real Michaud raised one hell of a kid.

To see full interviews of
some of the stars in this book
visit:

WWW.WFGSTARS.COM

Real Michaud

Real Michaud grew up in tiny town of 5,000 people in northern Alberta, Canada. His father worked for the government full time and worked part-time jobs to make ends meet. Real was industrious and started his first job at age 14 working in a men's clothing store. School didn't appeal much to young Real, and he skipped through most of high school to work. He dreamed of being his own boss someday. After high school, Real spent the next four years working for a major Canadian bank. He later spent 10 years working in the retail clothing business until he opened his own jewelry store. For the next 16 years, Michaud struggled to make the store successful. After managing to save $90,000, he invested it all on a hot stock tip from a friend that made him an overnight millionaire. The stock grew his investment to $1.7 million. Unfortunately, it sank as fast as it rose, and Michaud lost every penny. In his mid-forties, he was forced to liquidate the jewelry store and hunt for a job. He tried various network marketing opportunities and entrepreneurial ventures, but nothing worked. Real was down on his luck and was forced to ask his dad to cosign a loan for $40,000 so he could purchase a mobile home. Just as he was about to declare personal bankruptcy, he was approached about the opportunity that would become WFG. He was 46 years old with five kids to feed, and he hoped that this was the answer to his problems.

Real earned $118,000 in his first year, more money than he had ever earned in a single year. He went on to become the biggest leader in Canada. Today, at 67 years of age, Real Michaud sits atop a WFG empire that's freed thousands of people from financial hardship.

The first time I met Real Michaud was in an elevator in Red Deer, Alberta, Canada. I had heard his name for years, but I'd never had the opportunity to speak with him. I was conducting a mental toughness training seminar for 700 associates on Real's team, and we were both headed to the venue. I liked him from the moment we met. Real is one of those people you immediately trust. We had a nice conversation before I went onstage. After the seminar I was signing books for Real's team, and many of them shared how grateful they were to be mentored by him and his leaders. So much of my inside information about WFG and its leaders has been gleaned this way. Because I'm an outsider, people see me as someone safe to confide in about their experience. Some of the leaders are more loved than respected, and others are more respected than loved. I will tell you in no uncertain terms that Real Michaud is both. His humility is exceeded only by his sincere desire to help people.

In the summer of 2017, I spoke to 700 top WFG leaders in Las Vegas and reconnected with Real. As always, he was friendly and gracious. Two days later, I saw him speak to 25,000 people in the Mack Center, and once again I was captured by his ability to connect with his audience. This is a special man with the gift of relatability.

Real's secret weapon is his wife and business partner, Claudette, whom he calls "the backbone of our business." Real is the front man while Claudette handles the money and oversees the business. Together they are one of WFG's best husband-and-wife teams.

If you're getting the idea that I'm a raving Real Michaud fan, you're absolutely right. And to further make my case, I submit two people as evidence: Corey and Cameron, Real's sons. Both have become very successful in WFG, and more importantly, they both embody their father's character. You can tell a lot about a man by the behavior of his offspring, and Cam and Corey do not disappoint.

Here are some of the best quotes from my most recent interview with Real Michaud:

"The secret to success in WFG is that there is no secret, however, here are a couple of things I'd suggest you do: show up to everything, including training, seminars, local events, conventions, and

be a student of the business. Understand recruiting, building, the WFG system and compensation plan."

"The best advice I could offer someone considering WFG is to give it a 3-month trial. Commit to 4-8 hours a week for 3-months and you will know if this opportunity is for you."

"WFG is not for everyone, but at least give it a try. I would rather say that I gave it an honest effort and it wasn't for me than to be sitting here 5-years from now and wondering what if?"

Ed Mylett

Ed Mylett was born in Boston and grew up in Diamond Bar, California, with three sisters. He describes his upbringing as lower middle class. His dad struggled with alcoholism, which left young Ed on edge.

Ed's dream was to play professional baseball, and for many years it looked as though he would. From 1990–93, he played for the University of the Pacific Tigers, an NCAA Division I team, where he became an All-American. When an injury ended his big-league dream, he sunk into depression. He lost his house and car. Embarrassed and ashamed, he took a six-dollar-an-hour job working at a home for boys. Not long after, he was introduced to the financial services industry, which initially did not excite him. The one thing that grabbed his attention was the competition. As a former athlete, Mylett resonated with the idea of getting back in the game. And after working with the kids at the boys' home, he grew to love the idea of helping people. The combination of helping families with their finances and competing with other agents was enough to convince him to join the business.

Ed didn't break any records in his first three years. He claims to have had a series of false starts, and he even considered quitting the business. Ed explains his lack of early success:

"My whole life, even in baseball, I always held a little back so I'd have an excuse when I failed."

For a character as bold as Ed Mylett, this shows an acute level of self-awareness. Looking at him today, it's hard to imagine this hard charger holding anything back. As a former athlete around Mylett's level, I can tell you that most of us fall into this trap. The difference is that Mylett was self-aware enough to recognize and transcend it. I've coached some of the best athletes in the world, and I can state with some authority that this level of psychological introspection is rare.

Once Mylett decided to let loose, he became a force of nature and experienced tremendous success. He now serves as the WFG's agency chairman, and he speaks to and coaches the company's teams across the United States and Canada.

Mylett claims to be an introvert, but you wouldn't guess it from watching him onstage or on social media. You'll see him driving his Ferrari, walking off of his jet or relaxing in his oceanfront mansion in Laguna Beach.

Ed's philosophy is "max out," which is fitting for a guy with unbridled ambition. With the possible exception of Eric Olson, Ed is an anomaly in WFG. Some people love his style, and others feel it's over the top. He's intense, focused and driven. He makes no apologies for his success or style, and whether you agree with it or not, it's refreshing.

According to other leaders I interviewed, you don't have to be as driven as Mylett to become successful in WFG. There are lots of leaders with more modest levels of ambition and intensity. You'll find all kinds of different stars in this organization.

Ed Mylett is an important figure in WFG. He's helped thousands of associates take their businesses to the next level, and his aggressive style has pushed people to reach higher than they ever imagined they could.

Xuan Nguyen

Xuan Nguyen is one of the co-founders of WFG and grew up in Vietnam. His father died when he was 16, and the war in Vietnam pitted two of his brothers against each other. Xuan eventually escaped Vietnam in an unseaworthy small boat and was later rescued at sea by the American 7th Fleet. He ended up in Hawaii and later moved to California. He worked on an assembly line in Silicon Valley while attending night school. He later accepted a job as a social worker in job development helping other refugees from Vietnam get settled and find employment. Xuan did this for 10 years, and while he enjoyed the work, he wasn't earning enough money to support his growing family. He promised his wife that after she had the couple's third child, she could stay home and raise the children full time.

Xuan attempted to get into the insurance business, but no one would allow him to work the business part time. He couldn't afford to leave his full-time job for commission-based sales. As fate would have it, he was approached in the hallway of his office building by a woman who said her company was looking for people. Xuan accepted her invitation to attend the Business Presentation Meeting and at the end was offered a $5 starter kit. He didn't have the $5, so he asked the woman who invited him to loan it to him.

Soon after, Xuan started the business part time, and his closest contacts all rejected him. It took him four weeks to sign his first recruit. He continued working the business part time for two and a half years and in 1987 decided to pursue it as a career.

Today Xuan Nguyen is the most successful associate in the history of World Financial Group.

Xuan's hierarchy represents about half of the company's business. He's an iconic figure in this organization. He created his own system and holds his own events. World System Builders, Xuan's organization, is like a company within a company. The approach is a little different, but the focus on using systems to build the business is the same. I've interacted with thousands of Xuan's people, and they are among the friendliest and most genuine WFG associates.

As an outsider observing Xuan behind the scenes, I believe a large part of his success can be attributed to his philosophy of simplicity. Many of the traditional corporate leaders I've worked with seem to thrive on complex approaches to solving problems, but not Xuan Nguyen. His genius is rooted in his uncanny ability to reduce the fundamentals of the business down to its most simplistic form. In his own words, Xuan stated:

"You need a common denominator that people can rely on and a platform on which people can stand. The system must be simple, clear, fast and easy."

Nguyen realized years ago that people didn't always follow a leader, but they would follow a system. He said:

"We built a system for people to unify behind, instead of unifying behind me."

In the world of Xuan Nguyen, the system is the star as opposed to the leader. Whereas many leaders would prefer to bask in the glory of building a personality-driven business, Nguyen prefers to rely on the system and make it the hero. This is not only egoless and intelligent; it's a superior strategy.

It would be impossible to overestimate the impact and influence that Xuan Ngyuen has had on this company. And with that much power, it's important for you to know how he wields it. This may be best described in Xuan's own words:

"I love this business because of the people I work with. There are so many good people in this company. We are united by a dream and a mission, and the future for the next generation of associates is 10 times better."

Eric Olson

ERIC OLSON

When Eric James Olson was born in San Jose, California, on February 27, 1982, no one knew this gentle giant would one day shake the rafters of the financial services industry. Olson was a decent student but a standout athlete, lettering in multiple sports in high school. At 6'5" and 325 pounds, he was a beast on the gridiron and eventually attended NCAA Division I San Jose State University on a football scholarship. Olson would later become the Spartans' team captain. NFL scouts hovered, and Olson was offered a practice squad contract to play in the pros. During this time, the towering offensive guard was working at the San Jose Airport as a cashier at the tollbooth parking lot, earning $28,000 a year. Between his studies, football practices, part-time job and traveling around the country for games on the weekends, the ambitious Olson was burning the candle at both ends. One day during his junior year, his fiancée approached him to take a look at a business opportunity. Olson signed on immediately but had little time to devote to WFG. He earned $8,000 in commissions in the first 14 months. Around that time, he was invited to fly to Atlanta to watch a presentation by Ed Mylett. During the presentation, Mylett talked about his college baseball experience and his dashed dreams of playing in the major leagues. He talked about how WFG became his new game and how he channeled his athletic prowess into a successful career. Olson connected to Mylett's story and got excited. He flew back to San Jose and quit college, the football team and his job at the airport. Bold moves by a bold man.

In fairy tales, the rest of the story is poetic. But Olson's journey to the top, while epic, was nothing close to happily ever after. Preparing to set up shop full time with WFG, he announced his plans to his fiancée, who by then had soured on the business and told Olson in no uncertain terms that he would fail. The big man didn't take it well and immediately ended the couple's engagement. So, at age 21, Eric Olson set out to stake his claim.

And then failed to pass the license exam.

Undeterred, he hit the books harder and passed on his second try. Olson explains what happened next:

> *"I made WFG my sport. I started working 16-hours a day, 7-days a week. I went nuts. I was working like an animal."*

Ready to attack his warm market, Olson shared WFG with an uncle, who immediately found a negative article about the company and sent copies to all of Eric's relatives. Olson was devastated. When he quit the football team, his teammates started telling people he had joined a cult. Friends he had counted on rejected him. It was not the smooth foray into this new venture he had hoped for. Even his love life was suffering due to his 24/7 obsession with WFG. In our interview, Olson explained:

> *"When you want to conquer the world, when you're a crazy beast, it takes a special person to be with you. I had a lot of break ups."*

Obstacles aside, Olson powered through and earned an impressive $55,000 in commissions his first full–time month in the business. Not bad for a 21-year-old kid.

In his effort to attain new licenses and expand his offering, he failed seven more exams in the process. He finally buckled down in his studies and passed them all.

His first year as a full-time associate, Olson earned $251,000. And with a new level of confidence, he doubled his income the very next year to $500,000. In the third year, he doubled it again and hit a cool million.

In 2017, Olson's income skyrocketed to over $5 million.

I asked him to share some of his secrets to success in WFG:

"Some people recruit to the head, others to the heart. If a prospect is an action person, they want to see the houses and cars. The heart people want to hear about the crusade we have to help families with their finances. The technical people want to know the system."

Makes sense to me. Olson is known for using his Rolls-Royce, Ferrari and hillside home to market his success to new recruits. It's a strategy that some associates love and others loathe, yet it's hard to argue with its effectiveness. In the summer of 2017, I attended a backyard party at Olson's stunning San Jose home, and the tour included a driveway full of high-end automobiles. Olson explained:

"We're selling the dream", Olson explained. People want to see that there's money in the business."

As I sat through the party that night at age 52, the overt display of wealth seemed a bit much. After all, I had interviewed hundreds of the wealthiest people in the world, and most of them played down their wealth. But then I remembered the 20-year-old me back in 1984, when I would have thought those fancy cars were the coolest things in the world. What turns me on now in my fifties is being a vendor to a company that really helps people financially. After all, I've traveled the world, earned my fortune and understand the need the average person has for financial literacy. But back in the eighties, I was just a kid who wanted to be rich, and Olson's strategy would have been the only thing that would have grabbed my attention. So I decided to stop being a hypocrite and start appreciating this flamboyant approach to recruiting. I spoke with Eric about this more than a year later, and here's what he told me:

"I find out what their dreams are, and then I sell them back to them."

Genius, I thought. I mean, what's wrong with that? I felt my self-righteousness slipping away. Olson wasn't finished:

"If you recruit them with the crusade, they don't go full-time. I want them full-time. That's why I have so many full-timers. The older people are more into the crusade. I want to recruit them at 25-35 years old so I can override them for 40-50 years."

At first I thought Olson's approach sounded coldhearted. Upon further reflection, I concluded that it was the strategy of a man who knows what he wants and where he's going. Besides, I realized, I was one of those old people he was referring to! When I asked him for any final thoughts on his flashy recruiting tactics compared to other WFG leaders, he said:

"What makes our company great is all of the different styles. We all have different ways of doing the business."

Fair enough.

I moved on and asked Eric what he believed was the downside to the WFG opportunity. This was his response:

"People get excited, and then they realize that they have to work. It's not a get rich quick scheme. Most people are programmed to be an employee, and in WFG, you don't have a boss or manager. You have to be a self-starter and you have to be disciplined. You have to learn how to set your own schedule."

Eric's team currently has between 6,000–7,000 licensed agents, and they have collectively recruited over 100,000 people. I asked him how he did it:

"You have to train people, and training is the dirty work. We're not in the financial services business, we're in the leadership development business."

Olson continued:

"I have a huge vision, and my whole team is behind it. We love Art Williams, but we're going to beat him. We're going to create 1,000 millionaires. It's not about the money; it's about winning. I want to be the #1 team in financial services. I want to be a billionaire."

I guess one can conclude that with Eric Olson, it's not all about the money, but the money is still a strong motivator. I asked him what his goal was for 2018:

"I want to make $10 million dollars."

My last question during our interview was to ask Eric if he had any advice for someone considering WFG:

"Give it 18-months and then decide if you want to pursue it. Make your very best effort and then decide."

Eric Olson is something of an anomaly in WFG. His youth, success and unbridled ambition make him a unique and powerful leader. I've observed him in action for several years, and while he has his critics, no one can deny his herculean work ethic or his results. I've shared the stage with him in his home office in San Jose many times, and his people love him. He's created a culture of his own within WFG, and to say that it's an aggressive culture is an understatement. Before I met him, I was warned that he likes you only if you're on his team, but I didn't find that to be the case. He's hosted two of my seminars over the past two years, and he and his wife, Sandra, were extremely gracious and hospitable. Perhaps Sandra softens the rough edges of this billionaire-seeking beast. I refer to him that way with humor and affection. After my wife and I spent time with them as a couple, we agreed they're a perfect fit.

During my years of observing WFG leaders and conducting personal interviews with the leaders for the past six months, Eric Olson emerged as the most colorful character. The more his name came up during interviews, the deeper I dug into my research on him. My conclusion at the end was the same as it was the day I met him many years ago: I like Eric Olson. I respect his ambition and work ethic. But more importantly, I *understand* him. I've spent most of my life with hypercompetitive world-class performers, and they're a different breed. If you've never been one, it's impossible to understand the fury and fire that rages within. They can appear cold and calculating, but that's simply a side ef- fect of their ambition. They don't just *want* to win; they *need* to win. All obstacles must give way or be annihilated. It's not something they choose; *it's something they are.*

To see the full video interview with Eric Olson, visit
www.WFGSTARS.com

Siebold speaking to Eric Olson's Team Pinnacle in the studio at the Bona Allen Mansion

Penney Ooi

PENNEY OOI

Penney Ooi was born and raised in Malaysia and migrated to the United States in search of higher education and opportunity. She received a finance degree from Southern Illinois University and set out to stake her claim in the financial services industry. After being turned down by Merrill Lynch and other traditional companies, Penney was eventually approached about the oppor- tunity that would become WFG. Ooi didn't jump at her first in- vitation. It took eight for her to finally agree to attend the Business Presentation Meeting.

After coming on board in 1994, Penney earned $100,000 her first year in the business. Years later she would credit hard work and discipline as the cornerstones of her early success. By the end of her third year in the business, Penney was earning over $500,000. Her husband, Ben, an engineer, became her full-time business manager after that, which further fueled her meteoric rise to the top. In 2018, at age 50, Penney and Ben earned over $4 million per year as a field chairman with World Financial Group.

I've known Penney Ooi for many years, dating back to 2004 when I met her at a WFG event. She is humble, soft spoken and fiercely focused. As I've watched her business explode over the years, she has remained the same modest and genuine person. While some leaders allow their egos to get the best of them, Penney and Ben seem unaffected by their world-class success. Last year I conducted a mental toughness training seminar in San Jose, California, for 1,000 people on Penney's team, and the audience was impressive. Penney seems to attract high-level, humble, entrepreneurial people like herself. During my book signing with the team, I had the chance to have brief conversations with more than 400 of these leaders. What struck me most about Penney's people was the love and respect they have for their leader.

In 2018, I interviewed Penney at the Bona Allen Mansion, and I was moved by her humility and focus on helping her team. With Ben overseeing the business and Penney as the leader everyone wants to follow, the future for this dynamic duo is limitless.

To see the full video interview with Penney Ooi, visit www.WFGSTARS.com.

Siebold interviewing Penney Ooi in the ballroom of the Bona Allen Mansion

Bryce Peterson

BRYCE PETERSON

Bryce Peterson is one of the co-founders of WFG and was born and raised in the tiny town of Delta, Utah, during the 1950s and '60s. His par- ents worked hard but struggled financially. Bryce attended Utah Valley University in Orem, Utah, and received an associate's de- gree in marketing and business. After college, he went to work for Grand Central, a discount department store based in Salt Lake City. In 1977, he decided to join his uncle in the insurance busi- ness and quickly became the general agency's number-one salesman. One day Bryce was approached by Mark Redman, a fellow salesman at the agency, about a new opportu- nity in insurance sales. Bryce was reluctant to leave his uncle's firm but was attracted to this new way of doing business. Mark left the agency and signed on with the company that would lat- er morph into WFG, and Bryce followed shortly thereafter. He hoped it would be the chance of a lifetime, and his intuition was dead on. In 1979, after two years at his uncle's general agency, he was ready for his big opportunity. By 1985, Bryce was earning over $500,000 per year. By 1993, his income had skyrocketed to over $1 million per year.

Bryce Peterson is one of the few people currently still working in WFG who was there in the beginning. And as they say in New Jersey, he knows where all the bodies are buried. This is one of the reasons I was eager to interview him.

I met Bryce many years ago, the first time at a WFG leadership meeting in Las Vegas. I liked him immediately. He's an excep- tionally intelligent, charismatic man. I was fortunate to address his team multiple times over the years. One of the attributes that attracts people to Bryce is his lack of pretense. He says it like it is, and you can bank on his word. Today, at 64 years old, he's still plugging away at the opportunity that changed his life, and his excitement about the future of WFG is palpable.

"I love this profession. I love what we do," proclaims Peterson.

"All of the new financial products are amazing. It's so much better to-day than it was before. You can't even compare the past of this industry to the present, and it's only going to get better."

I asked him if it was easier to make it in WFG today than it was in the past:

> *"It's easier. In the beginning, all we had was term insurance. We told clients to buy term and invest the difference. Today there is so much more to offer. Today we are more of a financial advisory. And there are more bonuses than ever."*

One of the most inspiring parts of this interview was Bryce's energy and enthusiasm for the opportunity, especially considering that he's been at it for nearly 40 years. I asked him what he was most excited about:

> *"Steve, I have police officers earning $100,000 in their first year. That's exciting. I have my kids in the business and they're doing well. You don't bring your family into a business unless it's a great thing."*

Bryce was excited, so I decided to put him on the spot and ask him a question that's almost impossible to answer. After all, I thought to myself, he arguably has more experience than anyone actively working in all of World Financial Group. I wasn't sure if he would answer, but I knew I needed to ask. I said, "In today's WFG, with all of the great products, culture and compensation, how long would it take a brand-new associate to go from zero to a million dollars a year?" And he said:

"That's hard to answer, because there are so many variables to consider, but I would say that if someone really digs in and goes to work, they might be able to get there in 5-years."

Now, you might expect this kind of answer from a typical leader in an MLM company. But Bryce Peterson is not your typical leader, nor is he known for hyperbole. That's why I asked him this question. And he didn't take it lightly.

You might doubt that Peterson is right, but I would caution you against writing off his opinion. A man of his character and experience doesn't make statements without being aware of the potential consequences. I would humbly suggest that you temporarily suspend your disbelief and imagine what your life would be like if you could be earning a seven-figure income in five years. What would your life look like? How would it feel to be living an unrestricted existence like Bryce Peterson and his WFG comrades? Even if you see this as a stretch of your imagination, it's something to consider. Opportunities of this magnitude don't come along every day. When was the last time a multimillionaire like Bryce Peterson offered to mentor you in his business for free? I don't know about you, but I've never received a call like that. Most of us never will.

My final question for Bryce was in reference to the marketing approach that he employs, and after observing him for so many years, I figured I knew what he would say:

"The flashy approach can't be the core of recruiting. It attracts a lower level prospect. It's needs to be about more than money and recognition. WFG is about helping families understand how to create wealth and keep their money secure. It's not about material possessions. It's about serving and helping others have a better life."

James Schwartz

James Schwartz grew up in Maine, the son of a lobster fisherman and homemaker. He learned the lessons of hard work helping his dad out on the open sea, lessons that would one day make him wealthy.

After graduating from high school, James joined the Army and later served in Iraq from 2003 to 2005. After returning to the United States, he resigned his commission after 10 years of active duty. But once he left the military, James found himself drifting. He had dreams of becoming an entrepreneur, and after reading the book Rich Dad Poor Dad by Robert Kiyosaki, he decided to try his hand at the real estate business. He eventually purchased a Century 21 franchise in Dallas and became successful. James still felt like something was missing, and when an alarm salesman came into his office to sell him a system, fate seemed to step in. James rejected the offer, but before walking out the door, the salesman pitched him on looking at a new opportunity. James wasn't interested until the salesman said, "Robert Kiyosaki recommends it." This piqued James's interest enough to attend the Business Presentation Meeting and sign up on the spot. He closed his Century 21 office shortly thereafter. James explains:

"Deron Ferrell led the meeting, and he talked about what WFG does for families. He talked about WFG's mission, which is no family left behind. After that I knew that this was what I wanted to do."

Not everyone agreed with his decision, but James pushed forward and earned over $100,000 in his first 16 months. He credits much of his early success to the leadership training he received in the military:

"I was used to running systems, and I had a strong work ethic. Those things gave me a major advantage."

Since those early successes, James has risen to the CEO level in the company, ranking him among the most successful field leaders.

I had met James at WFG events over the years, but I didn't really get to know him until last year. I was immediately impressed with his sincerity. As an author and speaker, I meet around 100,000 people per year during my tours, media appearances and book signings. When you meet that many people, you develop a keen intuition, which makes it easy to identify people's motives. From our initial conversation, it was obvious that James believed in what he was doing and the company providing him with the opportunity. He's a powerful leader devoid of pretense. After spending a few hours with him, I understood why he is so successful.

James shared a story with me that sums up his value system. I asked him about WFG's culture, and he said:

"Family. That's the first thing that comes to my mind. When my Mom died, Joe DiPaola, (President/CEO of WFG) called me to see how I was doing and offer his condolences. Now imagine that. WFG has 60,000 agents and the President of the company calls me? That doesn't happen very often in traditional companies."

He's right. I've never heard of anything like that happening. This is part of the company's culture that fosters a level of loyalty about which most organizations can only dream.

To see the full video interview with James Schwartz, visit www.WFGSTARS.com.

Rocky Shi

Rocky Shi was born and raised in China, where both his mother and father are medical doctors. Young Rocky came to the Unit- ed States to study geology and later earned a PhD in civil en- gineer- ing from Johns Hopkins University. During his six years at Johns Hopkins, Rocky developed a keen interest in finance after taking a course on the subject. After completing his dissertation, he ac- cepted a position at Citibank, where he spent three years.

During this time, he was approached about the business, yet he had little understanding about how life insurance worked. Be- cause he had a love for working with numbers, he was imme- di- ately attracted to the opportunity. After attending a Business Presentation Meeting in 1996, he was so enthused that he stayed awake thinking about it until four a.m.

Rocky decided to become a part-time associate, building it on nights and weekends, along with his full-time job. By 1999, he was earning over $75,000 per year, and he decided to pursue the busi- ness full time. In the next 12 months, his income soared to over $100,000 per year. Even with this level of success, Rocky claims that he was "not a people person" and that he "didn't know how to be a leader."

Today Rocky Shi leads a massive team of WFG associates who manage over 100 offices in 26 states. He has seven leaders who earn in excess of $1 million per year. It's one of the accomplish- ments of which he is most proud.

For the past 13 years, I've watched Rocky build his empire. He's one of the most focused and sincere people I've ever known, and there was no doubt in my mind that he would become a force to be reckoned with in World Financial Group.

But there's more to the Rocky Shi story than meets the eye. Obvi- ously he's a smart, savvy businessman with an immigrant's ambition and discipline. No one who understands high-performance personalities would bet against this guy. There's an underlying quality to this man that shines through: integrity. When Rocky makes a promise, he always comes through. Here's a behind-the-scenes story you won't read on the Internet or anywhere else.

In 2007, Rocky called and asked me to conduct a Mental Toughness seminar for his team in Chicago. He said:

> *"Steve, we love your* 177 Mental Toughness Secrets *book, and we want you to come to Chicago and speak to the team. I will have over 900 people at the meeting."*

So I said, "Sure, I'd love to do it, Rocky." And then I told him my fee was $10,000. He said, "Steve, we don't have $10,000, but we will buy 900 copies of your book." I explained as nicely as I could that I'd need to charge him an additional $5,000 even if he purchased the books, and then he said:

> *"Steve, we don't have the $5,000, but someday, when I am rich, I will pay you back."*

Now, I'll be honest: I used to get offers like this all the time, and I always had to turn them down. I'm in business, I have employees to feed, and I need to make a profit to stay in business. But somehow I couldn't resist Rocky's offer. So I went to Chicago, delivered the seminar and signed 900 copies of my book for Rocky's team. They were wonderful, and I enjoyed it. I ended up losing money on the deal, but after I spoke, Rocky promised me again that someday he would pay me back.

Fast-forward 10 years to 2017. I'm in Maryland speaking to Andy Nguyen's WFG team, and Rocky asks me to stop by his meeting, which was being conducted in the same hotel. Along with WFG president Joe DiPaola, I addressed the group of 1,500 associates for a few minutes. Afterwards, I headed to my book signing in the hotel lobby and Rocky chased me down the corridor. He caught up with me and said, "Steve, remember in Chicago when I said I would pay you back when I was rich?" Honestly, I had forgotten about it, but when he brought it up, I remembered. So I laughed and said, "I do, Rock!" And he said, "I'm rich now." And he handed me an envelope, said thank you and walked away. I thought he was kidding, but I opened the envelope, and inside was a check for $5,000.

A different kind of leader would have given me the money on-stage in front of his team. As a matter of fact, I probably would have done it that way. But not Rocky Shi. He has too much class. Only he and I saw this exchange. It was one of the most impressive things I've experienced with this company. And in my opinion, it tells you everything you need to know about this man.

To see the full video interview with Rocky Shi, visit www.WFGSTARS.com.

John Shin

JOHN SHIN

John Shin's parents immigrated to the United States from South Korea so their children could receive a quality education. Growing up in Southern California, John and his sister were the only Asians in their neighborhood. John struggled in school as a child. He didn't understand English well, and he was thought to have a learning disability. Small in stature, John was the victim of re- peated bullying. This was a time when bullying was frowned upon by some and by others considered a rite of passage. John's experience would lead him to study martial arts, and he eventu- ally became a national champion.

His parents expected him to become a doctor or lawyer, and since he didn't like the idea of being around germs and blood, he chose to study law. This is where he met his wife, Arlene, and the couple married in 1994. Unbeknownst to John, Arlene entered the financial services business part time that same year. It took her a full year to tell John. She was earning a little money, and John thought, "If we both made that much money, we could pay off our student loans even faster." The problem was that John wasn't interested in finance and wasn't sure it was something he could even learn. He explains:

> "I wasn't one of those smart Asian kids. I scored a 640 on the SAT test, and they give you 400 for filling out your name! That gives you an idea of my intellectual ability."

Humility is part of Shin's charm, but the man has an MBA and a law degree from USC, so I'll let you draw your own conclusions.

He continued:

"Arlene asked me to go to Vegas. I thought we'd gamble and have some fun. Come to find out it's a convention for this company. I refused to go to the meeting for the first few days, but I agreed to attend the awards gala on Friday night. Not because I wanted to, but I had run out of money to gamble. I attended the next two days of meetings and that was it. Two weeks later I quit my job and went full time in the business."

I asked him how he did the first year.

"We made over $75,000 our first year."

Not bad for a guy who didn't think he was smart enough to understand finance. But the story was just beginning. John Shin would go on to become a household name in WFG, earning millions along the way. His empire now stretches across the United States and Canada. In the words of Ron Burgundy, the character portrayed by comedian Will Ferrell in the hit movie Anchorman, John Shin is "kind of a big deal."

I asked him about his secrets to success.

"You've got to have big dreams. Most people's dreams aren't big enough. Your dreams have to be so big that your brain has stretch marks."

Knowing John's impressive résumé, I wondered why he chose WFG. After all, this is a guy with a law degree and an MBA. Why would he spend all that time in school, not to mention the money attaining advanced degrees from a world-class university, and then join a network marketing company? I asked him, and this was his reply:

"One of the reasons I joined WFG was to gain financial literacy. We can blame everyone else, but in the end we have to take responsibility for the choices that we make. That's why I love WFG. It's teaching people about how money works at the elementary level."

I asked him to address the criticism that WFG receives about being a scam, cult and pyramid scheme:

"Only in the United States can people get away with saying things that aren't true. Most of what you read on the Internet is opinion, not fact. If a guy like me, who had a 1.9 GPA in high school, can make millions of dollars with this company, how can you say that it doesn't work or that it's a scam? I look at WFG as my payroll company. It's almost like a union where we all come together to gain greater buying power. WFG puts the training, compliance and infrastructure in place. That's what the company brings to the table. It brings tremendous value. It's similar to a McDonald's franchise in that you buy into their infrastructure. They have a system in place."

When it comes to WFG being accused of being a cult, he said:

"Each office is independently owned and operated, and you can motivate your team any way you like. It's about teamwork and camaraderie. It's about celebrating a promotion or when someone closes a big transaction. It's no different than a team sport. We don't think anything of the celebrations in sports, but when it's done in business, we think its weird and we call it cultish. Wal-Mart, Apple and Google do the same kind of thing. If your company isn't doing something to celebrate, you're probably with the wrong company."

This was one of my favorite answers in this interview. He's right. Corporate America is moving in this direction. It transforms a company into a community. People quit companies, but communities are full of friends. People are less likely to walk away from people to whom they have an emotional connection. It occurred

203

to me in that moment that creating a cultlike culture at WFG was a lightning bolt of brilliance. The critics may be right in that it appears to be a cult. However, that's also the glue that holds it together. The WFG culture of excessive recognition, dream-building and excitement elevates it beyond a business. It's a lifestyle, a place where you can get multiple wants, needs and dreams fulfilled under one roof. People who laugh at this company and its culture don't get it. It's like laughing at Albert Einstein as he explains his theory of relativity. The joke's not on WFG but on the critics who fail to understand its genius. And make no mistake: "genius" is the right word. This is a company that paid out over $750,000,000 in commissions in 2017.

In an industry that plays checkers, WFG is playing chess.

I asked John for his take, after being in the business for nearly a quarter century, on leaders who employ the hard sell to recruit people. This was his response:

> *"The offices that use hard-sell closes don't understand the business yet. They want to get a recruit just to say they got one. We refuse to allow people to sign up at the first meeting. We tell them to go home and discuss it with their spouse. We won't even process their paperwork after they sign up until they've attended at least three meetings."*

I asked him about the downside to the WFG opportunity.

> *"Like any business, you've got to front load it. You've got to give it all you've got. Most people don't. The hardest thing for most people in WFG is changing their habits. You have to make the necessary sacrifices in the beginning."*

But enough with the negative, I thought. So I asked John what has been his greatest joy in the business.

"People always say that they got into WFG to help people. For me, honestly, I had no desire to help nobody! (He laughs) When I joined WFG, it was all about me. I was selfish. I had to pay my bills. I had student loans and credit card debt. We lived in a studio apartment with 4 walls and I wanted to buy my wife a house. Now my greatest joy is taking someone with a burning desire and helping him or her reach their potential."

World Financial Group is chock-full of rags-to-riches stories. I asked John which was his favorite:

"I would say Jaime Villalovos. She grew up with 5-sisters in Medicine Lake, Montana, population 200. At 21, with no college degree, she leaves this little town for the bright lights of Los Angeles to go after her dream. Now she's living it."

Shin's right. Villalovos ranks among WFG royalty. She's a powerhouse and one of the company's most popular leaders.

As the interview was coming to a close, I asked John to offer his best advice to people considering WFG:

"WFG is not the best company for everyone. If you feel like this is the right opportunity for you; then do it. Don't take someone else's word. Find out for yourself. Everyone around me told me not to do it. What if I would have listened? Where would I be now? The friends that told me not to do it are in exactly the same place they were 24- years ago."

He continued:

"Give this business at least 2-years. You're not going to get good in 6-months. It's like golf. It takes time and practice. Eventually you build skills and get better. You have the muscles to succeed. You just have to learn how to use them."

And then he was back on the plane, headed home to Los Angeles, back to the dream life he'd built with Arlene and their family. Not bad for a kid from Korea who was underestimated and bullied. They used to laugh at little John Shin. No one's laughing now.

To see the full video interview with John Shin, visit www.WFGSTARS.com.

Siebold interviewing John Shin in the studio at the Bona Allen Mansion

Gregg Strynadka

GREGG STRYNADKA

Gregg Strynada was born in 1980 and grew up an aspiring hockey star in Edmonton, Alberta, Canada. He played junior hockey in British Columbia but moved back to Edmonton to join the family business. Gregg's parents operated a juice and smoothie franchise, and Gregg soon found himself working long hours for little money and even less satisfaction. At 22, he signed on with World Financial Group. He struggled the first year and earned around $12,000. Gregg admits that he thought about quitting many times but eventually decided to forge ahead. Gregg ex- plains:

"It took me 12-18 months to get good."

In Gregg's second year in the business, his income soared to over $68,000, a staggering sum for a 23-year-old who had never earned more than $27,000 in a single year. Gregg was excited and more motivated than ever, and as fate would have it, his dreams of financial success were about to become reality.

In his third year, Gregg earned $129,000, and by the end of his seventh year in WFG, he had earned in excess of $600,000. Not bad for a 29-year-old former hockey player turned smoothie operator.

And he was just getting started.

Now 15 years in the business, Strynadka has become a household name in WFG-land. His income has skyrocketed to well over $1 million per year, and his hierarchy recruits over 2,000 people a year.

I interviewed Gregg in May of 2018, and he seemed as excited about WFG now as he was when he started out in the business 15-years ago. He's dynamic, enthusiastic and focused in his approach. At 38 years of age, Strynadka is well positioned to climb higher than ever over the next decade. I asked him to explain his WFG success strategies:

> *"Your business needs to be as simple as possible, with as few moving parts as possible, but still able to get the job done."*

I asked Gregg about his approach to and philosophy about recruiting. He said:

> *"Our philosophy is right down the middle. In other words, we sell the dream, but we also talk about the mission of helping families with their finances. I drive a Tesla, but flashy marketing is not my lead recruiting strategy."*

I wasn't surprised. In the land of hockey, Real Michaud and Raja Dhaliwal, you wouldn't expect Strynadka to be posing for pictures next to a private jet. That being said, he made a point not to downplay the role that dream-building plays:

> *"I want to recruit people who want more and are excited about our crusade."*

Moderation. Not surprising, coming from a Canadian. At the risk of stereotyping a great country of 37 million people, I say the Canadian style of moderation and straightforwardness breeds trust. And according to WFG cofounder Rich Thawley, trust is the core element of success in WFG.

When I pushed Strynadka for more strategies, he obliged:

"I teach my team to have a recruiting mentality, but training is just as important as recruiting. Your business will really grow when you have a whole bunch of people that can do it without you."

He continued:

"You have to be competent at the basic skills of the business, which are recruiting, selling, phone and presentation skills. Most people don't put the time into getting good at these basic skills. They have big aspirations, but they won't do the work. I learned my work ethic from the juice and smoothie business, where I was working from 60-100 hours per week and getting paid $2200 a month. You have to work hard and be mentally tough."

And there it was: mental toughness. If I learned anything after all of my years coaching world-class athletes, it's that they are all mentally tough. I'm guessing that he developed mental toughness from his days on the ice. Hockey players are among the most mentally and physically tough athletes. But while the majority of sports heroes fail to transfer their psychological prowess into financial success, Strynadka was able to capitalize on it. His success is now part of WFG history, but it couldn't have been all peaches and cream. I asked him about the biggest obstacles that he faced:

"Negative people in my life. My roommates and other friends told me it wasn't going to work and I was wasting my time."

When I asked him how he handled the barrage of criticism and negativity, he replied as any great athlete would:

"I turned it into fuel."

"Rocket" Richard would be proud. So would the Great One.

One of the things I've learned over my 30 years in business is that there's a downside to every deal. No matter how good something looks, there are roadblocks to consider before entering any business. I asked Gregg what he found to be the downside of WFG:

> *"It's not easy. At the end of the day, it's still hard work. It's two to three months before you make any money after you get licensed, and in Canada, that means investing 50 to 60 hours studying in front of a computer for the exam. That's one of the reasons only 15% of our people get licensed."*

My final question for Gregg was regarding his best advice for someone who might be on the fence about joining WFG:

> *"You'll never know if this could be for you unless you try. It's a couple hundred bucks. That's the worst-case scenario. That's all you have to lose."*

After Gregg said that, it occurred to me that it would be worth a couple hundred dollars just to meet this 38-year-old self-made millionaire. And for the opportunity to be mentored by him?

Well, that would be priceless.

SUBSCRIBE TO THE BLOG

www.mentaltoughnessblog.com

Haihong Sun

HAIHONG SUN

Haihong Sun came to the United States from China in 1999 with her husband to attend the University of Illinois. She received a five-year scholarship and graduated with a PhD in biophysics and computational biology. Her husband also graduated with a PhD. He went to work as a director of a large bank on Wall Street. During this time, a friend from China, with whom the couple had gone to school, introduced them to WFG. In 2002, the couple became clients. After attending the company's national convention in Las Vegas in 2003, they decided to join the business.

The first year, Sun earned $40,000 with WFG as a graduate student working part time. Today she oversees one of the largest WFG organizations in New York.

I asked her about what she sees as the downside of the business:

"People quit. Prospects don't always buy. You can't be addicted to other people's approval."

Haihong has the sunny disposition of a foreigner who's worked hard and made it big in her adopted homeland. She beams with excitement and gratitude when she speaks about WFG. I asked her what she says to people who call WFG a pyramid scheme:

"It's multilevel marketing, not a pyramid scheme. You need a mentor to teach and guide you, and this model pays them to do it."

This interview was the first time I had met Haihong. I had heard her name throughout the years but never had a chance to meet her face-to-face. I couldn't imagine her as a hard closer, but I felt compelled to ask her about how she felt about the hard-sell approach:

"Some agents hard sell, but not the experienced ones. I only recruit people who want to join. I only sell people who want to buy. If you ask people who have been in WFG for more than 5-years, they'll tell you that you can't hard sell. You can't retain people that you hard sell."

With Haihong's cheerful personality, I wondered if she ever experienced an emotional low point when she was building her business, and she said:

"At one of the conventions, I brought 10 people all the way from New York to Las Vegas to check it out, and 8 of them left."

During the research for this book, other leaders shared similar stories. The atmosphere in WFG's national conventions is unique, and it turns some people off. It's hard to explain what these meetings are like. Imagine 35,000 of the most excited, fired-up souls you've ever met jammed into an arena for four straight days and nights. These people see WFG as the opportunity of a lifetime, their golden ticket to financial freedom. I've experienced these conventions from backstage, onstage and way up in the nose-bleed section. To the casual observer, it may come across as someing like a secular tent revival, something so overflowing with positive energy that it could be perceived as a put-on. I understand when people new to WFG's culture react this way, but make no mistake: the excitement you see is no circus act. These people are genuinely excited, and they're not afraid to show it. These con- ventions are conducted, in this author's opinion, to show people the big picture and build their belief in the magnitude of the op- portunity. It's part educational seminar, part motivational pep rally and part opportunity showcase. And WFG spares no expense in doing it right.

Besides some people being turned off by the convention, I asked Haihong about the other obstacles she's encountered:

"We were naïve. We didn't have good people skills. Before I joined WFG, I was self-centered."

I asked Haihong what she, after 13 years in the business and with the wind at her back, would do differently if she started over:

"I'd be an even better student. This is a monkey-see, monkey-do business. If you do 90% of it right and 10% wrong, people will follow the 10%. I would also go on more field training appointments. I did about 20, but I should have gone on at least 50. The more field training you get, the more you can help your team."

I asked her about her favorite client story, and she said:

"I had a prospect I was trying to turn into a client who I had to follow up with 10 times before they purchased a policy. They were both Yale graduates. They asked lots of questions every time I met with them, but they didn't buy. It was four hours round trip every time I met with them. The person who called on them before me had given up, but I kept following up. They finally became clients and introduced me to one their friends, who got into the business and became one of our million-dollar earners"

As we concluded the interview, I asked her what advice she would offer someone considering WFG as a career:

"If our mission of helping families build and protect their wealth is something you believe in, you can make it in WFG. Give yourself enough time. Don't expect too much too fast. Don't think about the compensation for the first two to three years. Instead, think about how potentially huge your business can be."

It was great getting to know Haihong. She's exceptionally bright, and it's easy to see why people follow this Chinese-American star. As I reflected on our interview later that day, I thought about her story. When a person can come from a foreign land with little money or contacts and become a WFG millionaire, that's something special. Sure, it's a testament to her talent and tenacity, but without the WFG platform, it wouldn't have been possible. How can you credibly criticize an opportunity whereby Haihong's story is even possible?

To see the full video interview with Haihong Sun, visit www.WFGSTARS.com.

Siebold interviewing Haihong Sun in the studio at the Bona Allen Mansion

Rich Thawley

Rich Thawley is one of the original cofounders and the senior statesman and patriarch of World Financial Group. He was born in the early 1950s in Southern California. His dad was a general contractor, and the family eventually moved to Northern California to raise horses. Young Rich developed the world-class work ethic for which he would later be known by cleaning and maintaining 30 horse stalls alongside his brother. Rich's parents grew up during the heart of the Great Depression, and like most families of that era, they struggled to make ends meet. The lessons of living below your means and being fiscally responsible were drilled into Rich's head at an early age. Though the family didn't have a lot of money, Thawley says he never felt poor, and the years of living a simple life rank among his fondest memories.

The storybook marriage of Rich and Cindy Thawley began at San Jose State University when Rich walked into Cindy's sorority house to promote his candidacy for student government. As he describes it, it was love at first sight. The couple married in 1979 and moved into a mobile home three mobile homes down the road from his parents. He began working as an assistant athletic director at his alma mater, and Cindy worked as an administrative assistant. The couple decided that they eventually wanted to build a business together, yet at the time, they weren't sure what type of business it might be. They were just scraping by financially, and with Rich's conservative style, there was no telling how long it would take for this couple to set up shop. One day a friend of Rich who had played music at the couple's wedding invited him to a Business Opportunity Meeting. Rich explains:

"If I had a flash-bang, it was probably at that meeting. I saw something. I felt it. I got confirmation, and I trusted that feeling."

And a legacy was launched, a career that would eventually span all 50 states and 10 provinces of Canada. I asked Rich what he wanted from the business when he signed up.

"We started part-time to pay off our Visa card and get a couch", he says with a smile. "A few months later, we had $30,000 in savings."

I asked him what this huge leap in income was like:

"That was two years of my income. I can't tell you how excited we were. Two years later we had a million in savings. We were beside ourselves."

This is not a typical success story, and Rich Thawley will be the first person to admit it. While anything is possible, most associates do not experience such a thunderous rise. But Rich Thawley is no ordinary man. I've watched him behind the scenes for years, and he's what I would call a laser-focused workhorse. He's old-school mentally tough, the kind of toughness that was bred into the children of Depression-era parents, the kind of toughness you learn on the street. Rich describes the early years of building the business:

"We worked so hard that people thought we were crazy. I look at pictures of myself back then, and man, I look tired! But we were very consistent and we developed expertise and taught it to our team."

The 1980s were very good to Rich Thawley. Then came the '90s. A. L. Williams was sold, and Holm, Humphrey, Miles, Thawley, and the other leaders had to decide whether to stay with the new owner, Sandy Weill, or to blaze their own trail with a brand-new company. Resigning would cost them millions in collective residuals. This and other considerations made it a difficult decision. Rich shared the story of what put him over the top. He seemed uncomfortable in telling it, and afterwards I understood why:

"We're a company that was built with a lot of enthusiasm for recognition. We love making people feel special."

He went on to tell me the story of being at the head table during the first convention put on by the new parent company. The leaders had submitted a long list of people who were to be recognized at the event, and the new president refused to read off the names and bring them onstage. One leader was brought up and then rudely dismissed in front of an auditorium full of his peers. This did not sit well with Rich. He felt that this was the new company culture. He describes the scene:

"I leaned back in my chair and whispered to Cindy, that's it. We're out of here."

This was one of the highlights of the interview. I've heard Rich Thawley speak onstage many times about the importance of character, and now I got to see his up close. Imagine this then-40-year-old man walking away from a million-dollar income be- cause he didn't agree with the new company culture. This is a kid who came from nothing, and now he was giving up a life that most people would die for on principle? Come on, really? Yes. And that one decision made all the difference. I couldn't help being impressed. Then I reminded myself once again that Thawley was old school, raised with the same philosophy as I was by my own Depression-era parents. Thawley and I are both baby boomers, and there's a unique mindset that our generation was instructed to embrace. We were taught to always do the right thing, even if it costs you. The greatest generation didn't pull punches or mince words. You do it right or you don't do it. Mind your manners, clean your plate, and do your chores. You won't like the consequences if you don't. This was the generation that survived the Great Depression, fought in World War II and built the richest country in the history of the world. They saw and experienced things later generations couldn't imagine, and it made them tough. The children of this resilient generation can't claim the same level of grit, but the scars are forever etched in their consciousness. Knowing that Thawley possessed this mental toughness, I still wondered about the fear he must have felt from the moment he leaned over to Cindy to the time he helped co-found the new company. So I asked him, and this is what he said:

"Well, I had been happy in the mobile home before. You must know what to stand for. You must know what's important. Don't be dazzled by the other stuff. So we resigned our positions and laid it all on the line. We were committed all the way down to our wedding rings. It was sink or swim. Once you remove the options, it's pretty easy to go into attack mode. You need to have a little bit of fear motivating you — not the kind that paralyzes you but the kind that says, 'Get off your butt and get going.' It took us two years to get back to where we were before."

I thought to myself, Wow, that was gutsy to put it all on the line. I'm not sure I would have been able to do it. Talk about toughness. But the future wasn't all sunshine and roses. I asked Rich about the obstacles he and the other leaders faced along the way:

"You can't microwave a great company. You can't microwave a great family. It's got to be done over time. Leadership is hard work, and that doesn't happen overnight either. We have an entrepreneurial culture, and you have to help people transition from employee to entrepreneur. You have to teach them those disciplines and habits. It's not a nine-to-five. You have to teach people how to pay the price, and you have to teach them how to make promises and keep them."

Hard to argue with that, I thought. But I wanted to dig deeper into the personal struggles of a man who, when you see him on-stage, seems larger than life. I secretly wondered if he had always been Superman or if somewhere below the surface a young Clark Kent had formerly existed. As usual, Thawley was candid and on point:

"The first time I had to do a business presentation, there were six or seven people in the room. I was sweating profusely, like I had played four quarters of basketball. It was embarrassing. The first time I gave the talk, I was sitting in the car with Cindy. She said, 'Doesn't the meeting start at seven?' And I said, 'It's not seven yet.' She said, 'It's 6:59,' and I said, 'Yeah, but it's not seven.' She said, 'Oh, are they coming down to the car, or are we supposed to go up there?' And we were sitting in a two-seater! So we go up there, and I head straight for the bathroom. I remember looking in the mirror and seeing how pale I was and how much I was sweating. So I threw some water on my face and went in. I gave the presentation and don't remember any of it."

And this terror of public speaking went on for 16-months. Rich describes the agony:

"I was all butterflies. I couldn't eat within 3 or 4-hours of giving the talk. And that's after giving these talks multiple times a week. My stomach would be in knots, to the point where people would notice. But I circled the calendar on a Saturday morning when I gave the talk and was completely relaxed. If you face the fear, it eventually goes away."

If you've ever experienced the feelings of terror that public speaking can generate, it's no laughing matter. Instead of facing it head on, most people avoid it. I asked Rich what made him fight so hard to overcome his fear.:

"I fought the fight because I wanted to be somebody. I wanted to win. I wanted to win for Cindy, and for the family we hadn't started yet. I wanted to deliver for the team that expected me to deliver. We had a lot of people counting on us for leadership, and I knew they were watching everything we did. I knew that everything I did would be copied."

I finished this line of questioning by asking Rich about his biggest fear when he was getting started, and he replied:

"My biggest fear was that I'd lose my passion for it, just like I had for other things in my life. But I never have, and that's because I know how much we've helped people."

He's right. A lot of people claim to spend their lives helping people, but few have had the impact or reach of Rich Thawley. I know because I've had thousands of the people on his team attend my programs, and they've shared their stories with me. They love and respect this man.

Now, if you're new to WFG or a critic of the company, you might be saying, "Yes, and Thawley has become very rich in the process. He's been well compensated for his leadership and altruism." And you're right. Rich Thawley has made a lot of money in the business. But I'd ask you to consider the number of people in business who make millions and never help a soul along the way, the Gordon Gekkos of the world who proclaim that greed is good and that nothing is personal, only business. That's not Rich Thawley. If you think he did it only for the money, I've failed as an author to describe the heart of this giant. This is a man who cares more about people than prosperity. He was fortunate to find a business in which strong character and traditional values are the lifeblood.

Another aspect of Rich's approach to the business that impressed me was the level of caution and concern he expressed for his people. When I asked him about launching the new company, here's what he said:

"We wanted a company that could start people part-time, in the shallow end of the pool. We knew we could take everyone and throw them into the deep end, and the gifted would survive while everyone else drowned. So we started everyone in the shallow end. Our idea was, and still is, to keep everyone as safe as we can."

Being face-to-face with the cofounder of a company with 70,000+ licensed agents is a privilege, and not one that I take lightly. That being said, my duty is to you, the reader, to ask the questions to which you want the answers so you can make a quality decision about moving forward with these folks. So as I had asked the other leaders, I asked Rich Thawley to respond to the criticism that's been levied at both the leaders and the company. Thawley answered every question when he could have easily declined. As expected, he was honest and forthcoming. Here's how he responded to criticism in general:

"We wouldn't have gotten anywhere if I had caved into criticism. I was criticized legitimately plenty when I was coming up as a leader. There is legitimate criticism, stuff you have to square away, mistakes you've made, someone does something dumb. You have to make restitution, ask forgiveness and resolve not to make the mistake again. There's another kind of criticism, when people just get mad, and you have to learn to separate the two."

That made sense to me. After all, people love to criticize things they don't understand or things at which they fail. My being a lousy guitar player after 40 years of lessons can't be my fault, so I blame all of my teachers. It's their fault, so I take to the Internet and lambaste them for letting me down. As a matter of fact, I think guitar lessons are a scam, a cult and a pyramid scheme all rolled into one. They may even be illegal! I read it on the Internet, so it must be true, right? You see, by the time Rich Thawley showed up for our interview at the Bona Allen Mansion, I had interviewed over 100 people for this book. I had heard one coherent response after another that defused each and every criticism that I had researched online about the company. Simply put, I just wasn't buying it anymore. I knew at this point in the project that I possessed more inside information about the organization and the people who lead it than most of its 70,000 licensed agents. I calculated that I had invested well over 1,200 hours in the writing, interviews and related research over a six-month period, and my confidence was high. This mountain of research made me an even bigger believer, and now I had the proof I needed to back up my belief and present it to the world. With this in mind, I boldly but respectfully asked Rich about what he viewed as real and legitimate criticisms of WFG and the opportunity. Here's what he said:

> "*A legitimate criticism is that it's hard work. It's not easy, and it's not for the faint of heart. Any leader who says that it's a piece of cake, well, that's nonsense. I want people to have realistic expectations. It's also legitimate to say that a lot of people don't make it and that this is tough. You've got to strengthen yourself. It forces you to improve, but it doesn't happen overnight. If someone misled you by saying it's get rich quick, slap them! You have my permission.*"

Tough words from a tough guy, words you probably won't ever see on a WFG brochure or website. But they're honest words from a field leader who's seen it all. Every business has pros and cons no matter how noble or well-intended its people may be. Wheth- er or not you decide to join WFG, you'll know the naked and bru- tal truth. Now you know why this book had to be un-authorized. If it were filled with positive-thinking platitudes and gushing tes- timonials, it wouldn't be of much value. My goal was to take you behind the curtain so you could see the wizard for yourself. After that, you could draw your own conclusions. With this goal in mind, I asked Rich about some of the people he recruited who had quit:

> "*I recruited this guy whose only goal was to make $2,800 bucks so he could buy a flat screen television. So, he made the $2,800 bucks and quit. His leader called him and said why did you quit? And he said, I got my flat screen, and I'm watching it right now. That's why I did it.*"

Too funny, I thought. We both laughed. I saw this as a good time to ask another key question. I said, "If you had to do it all over again, is there anything you'd do differently?" He smiled warmly and said:

"That gets me excited just thinking about it, because today we have so much more earning power in our system."

Then he gave me a kind of reflective look and said:

"I was pretty tough on people, but Cindy tempered me. Then we had a daughter, and she softened my heart. I wasn't mean-spirited. My parents taught me right. But it was kind of a sports thing. The combination of the two made it work. I brought tough love, and Cindy brought the sensitive part until I got better. I learned compassion from my wife. But I had less trouble with compassion than I did with patience. I understood the responsibility of controlling my tongue. Art Williams said one time in a room full of his leaders that one word of encouragement can make someone's day on your team, maybe even change their life. One word of criticism or thoughtlessness and they go home devastated while you go home financially independent. It may even cost them the opportunity. Remember that you have a responsibility to control your tongue."

Rich's words as well as Art Williams's made me shriek. I too came from coaching great athletes, some of the world's best, and had been guilty of hammering them into submission. I later learned that while professional and Olympic athletes can handle the nastiest of tongue-lashings, this level of coaching makes the average person melt. I too, had been guilty of being tough on people who were untrained and emotionally ill equipped to endure it.

Rich continued:

"Remember how significant you can be in other people's lives. Sometimes you don't even know you're making a difference."

Rich began to get choked up. He fought back tears, and through a shaky voice, continued:

"A few years ago, a friend of mine and I were sitting next to a woman at the WFG convention, and the woman leaned over to him and said, 'Can I see your program? Do you know when Rich Thawley talks? I really like listening to him. One of his talks caused my husband to start coming back to church with our family, and it's changed everything."

Rich was visibly moved as he shared this story, and so was I. He continued:

"I don't know who this woman was and I'll never know. You just don't know when you stand up in front of a group of people; you have an opportunity to have an impact in a way that's meaningful. You want to embrace that."

We were getting close to the end of the interview. Rich had to catch a plane back to San Jose. I asked him if he had any regrets:

"There's a part of me that wishes we would have built it even bigger. I don't look back on my life with a lot of regret. Oh, sure, I wish I would have bought that stock or piece of real estate, but I accept the fact that I'm imperfect. I'm going to keep trying to do the right thing. If I knew how to build the perfect company, I would. Looking back, there's not a lot I would change. I'm looking forward to the next 20 to 25 years."

I asked Rich for his best advice for people building the business:

"Help others do things for themselves that they couldn't do without your help. If you can keep doing that, lots of good things are going to happen for you in this business. From a relationship-building

230

standpoint, the thing that matters most is trust. The moment trust leaves, love starts to fade, even in the best of circumstances. It's true in all of our relationships. The foundation of all relationships is trust. It's far more important that they trust you than it is that they like you, much less love you. And don't forget about character. The number-one reflection of our character is how we treat people."

My final question was an easy one for the powerful patriarch. I asked him what advice he would offer someone who was on the fence about signing on with the firm:

"When you're trying to weigh it, consider that when someone is dishonest, they always ask for something. We're not asking for anything. If we're just blowing smoke, you're going to know it in a day or two. So we've got to shoot straight with you, and we want you to know what's coming. It's not going to be easy. You're going to talk to friends, and they're going to tell you to take a hike. People are going to stand you up. And it may be your best friend from high school. These are things that happen, and if you can't take it, you'll quit. The good news is that we didn't ask you to quit your job, put your house up for sale or empty your savings account. Our whole goal is to help you see if you can build a business here, pure and simple, one piece at a time."

I shook Rich's hand and thanked him for coming to the Mansion and sharing his wisdom. Later that night, I was having dinner with my wife and reminiscing about the Thawley interview. She said, "I think you're becoming obsessed with this book." I shrugged it off and laughed. Upon further reflection, I realized she was right.

For 13 years, I had known and admired these people, their compa- ny and the opportunity. But after six months of digging into every nook and cranny, I knew far too much to remain a passive fan. It wasn't like I had given them a free pass and taken their word for everything they said. I checked and double-checked anything I suspected to be hyperbole, and it all checked out. It wasn't like I was searching for a smoking gun or a trail of corruption, but as a writer, I'm obligated to my readers to be open to the possibility. All I found was a group of well-intentioned, street-tough entre- preneurs solving problems for people while bettering their own lives—people like Rich Thawley.

My conclusion on Thawley is that he's a deeply committed man with a damn good heart, an introvert who beat the odds in an industry of extroverts.

To his legions of followers, Rich Thawley is a living legend. To me, he's just a good man trying to do the right thing.

I think he would be comfortable with that.

To see the full video interview with Rich Thawley, visit www. WFGSTARS.com.

Siebold and co-founder Rich Thawley in the studio at the Bona Allen Mansion

Micky Nguyen and Linh Truong

MICKY NGUYEN & LINH TRUONG

Micky Nguyen and Linh Truong are one of WFG's power couples. Both are originally from Vietnam and came to America after the Vietnam War. Linh first settled in Los Angeles and Micky in Virginia Beach. After graduating from college, Linh went to work as an underwriter for State Farm. She later opened a spa and nail salon and two dry cleaners. Micky worked as a mechanical engineer before launching into WFG.

Micky was attracted to WFG by the possibility of getting a financial education, making extra income and building his own business part time. His initially modest goals evolved into the dream of achieving financial freedom. Eventually Micky and Linh's success in WFG allowed them to help both of their parents retire. I asked Micky about some of the obstacles he faced during his ascent in the business:

> *"I was an introverted engineer, so I had to transform myself completely. I had to become more social, develop people skills and learn how to connect."*

But building the WFG business wasn't always smooth sailing:

> *"After several years of building, I lost about 80% of my licensed associates in one weekend to a copycat company while I was out of town."*

Despite the enormity of this setback, Micky continued to build. Today, the couple's business is thriving. None of the agents who left their team remain in the industry.

The incestuous practice of recruiting people from one MLM to another is common in this industry, yet it rarely works out long term. WFG has had a few defectors who have taken this route, yet none has produced any noteworthy success. Historically, these upstarts have made a lot of claims yet have produced only marginal results.

As I've expressed earlier in this book, one of the reasons WFG thrives is the strength of its culture. I asked Micky Nguyen about this:

"WFG's culture is unique because of our field leadership and all of the human capital that was invested many years ago by the original founders. These men are still fully involved in the business serving as mentors to the next generation of leaders. Our culture promotes family values, integrity and character."

I asked Micky what he would do differently if he had to start over with WFG, and he shared this:

"I would talk to more people faster. It took me a while to overcome my addiction to the approval of others. Eventually I realized that the fear of rejection was never going to go away, and I had to have a series of 60-second bursts of courage if I was going to become successful. It's the rapid and constant repetition of discomfort that leads to emotional desensitization."

One of the questions I like to ask leaders in WFG is about their favorite client story. While on the surface this may seem like a simple question, it's much more. The answer helps to uncover the value system of the leader. It gives you an idea of who someone is below the surface. Here's what Micky Nguyen said:

"If I had to pick one favorite client story, it's the passing of the main breadwinner due to an unexpected illness. He left behind a substantial death benefit for his wife, a homemaker with two young children. The proceeds were used to pay off the mortgage and to fund some investments, including college for the children."

Micky's answer is not uncommon in WFG. I've asked dozens of the company's biggest leaders this same question, and their answers are similar. I included this question in the interview in an effort to dispel one of the most common myths in multilevel/ net- work marketing, which is that its people are obsessed with mon- ey and material possessions.

Yes, there is an emphasis on gaining financial freedom. I've surveyed over 20,000 WFG associates in the past three years, and 99.8% of them cite financial independence as their primary reason for getting involved. But anyone who thinks getting rich is the driving force behind the most successful people is wrong. A higher, more inspirational calling drives the core group of serious, committed leaders. Micky and Linh are standouts among this group.

In the closing segment of our interview, I asked Micky what advice he would offer someone considering WFG:

"Conduct your due diligence, and look at all of the amazing success stories of good people from all walks of life, ethnicities, financial backgrounds and education."

Julio Velazquez

Julio Velazquez was born in Puerto Rico, the son of restaurateurs who owned and operated a small eatery. Julio grew up working with his parents and learning the business. One day when he was 19, he was chopping chicken when a neighbor's boyfriend approached him and asked, "Are you going to be chopping chicken for the rest of your life?" Julio recalls that the temperature that day was over 100 degrees, and the restaurant didn't have air-conditioning. Julio responded by saying, "I hope not." The man then invited him to an opportunity. Julio asked, "Is it legal?" The man said, "Yes. It has to do with insurance." Julio had seen insurance agents in his neighborhood. They drove nice cars and dressed well. So he decided to attend the meeting:

"The gentleman conducting the presentation said you could make $50,000 a year. That sounded like all the money in the world to me."

Julio asked his father for $200 to sign up. His dad was reluctant, but his mom said, "Give him the money for the pyramid thing so he will learn his lesson." Julio later asked his father for an additional $300 to get his license and for an appointment with his trainer. Once again, Mom stepped in and told his dad to give him the money so he could go through the process. One year later, he told his parents that he wanted to quit the restaurant and college so he could pursue his financial services business full time. His parents agreed to allow this if he got his securities license. The day he passed the exam was his last day of school. Julio's parents sold the restaurant shortly thereafter and moved to Connecticut to live near their daughter. They left 20-year-old Julio responsible for the house and all of the expenses, which came to $18,000 a year. He earned that exact amount in his business that year, just enough to stay afloat. He says with a smile:

"People ask me, how did I eat? And tell them that I ate at my appointments", he says with a smile. "I purposely booked all of my appointments at six p.m. when people were having dinner."

The next year, at age 21, the young entrepreneur earned an impressive $60,000. He earned a company ring and flew his parents in for the ceremony. He would spend 10 years at that firm, earning as much as $200,000 per year, before resigning his post. He had become disillusioned with what he saw as a faulty product, the same one his trainer had sold his mother when he first joined the business. His mother was upset with the product, and upon further study, Julio realized that what he had thought was suitable for her was actually a substandard product. The guilt for this unintended, unfortunate event drove him to cancel his insurance license and exit the industry.

Velazquez opened a tax training practice with a friend in Puerto Rico and began building the business. He soon realized that tax preparers and accountants were the perfect people to sell finan- cial services. He immediately began researching companies, and after several months, he remembered that World Financial Group had an office in Puerto Rico. He called the office, started asking questions and was told that WFG had been there for 20 years and had 14 agents. Knowing the industry, he asked for the leader's name in the United States, and the man gave him Deron Ferrell's number. It was February, and Ferrell and the other WFG stars were in Hawaii for their annual trip. When he reached him two weeks later, Velazquez told Ferrell that he had 10 years experience in the business and had decided to join WFG as long as he could believe in the product. Ferrell was more than happy to dissect the Indexed Universal Life Insurance Product, and Velazquez signed on.

He explains what happened in that first year:

"I earned $120,000 my first year with WFG. It's all about expecta-
tion. I knew I was worth at least that much. I knew that if I didn't
make at least $100,000, the system didn't work. With the skills and
knowledge I brought to the table, it wasn't that difficult."

Fast-forward to 2018. Julio Velazquez is an executive vice chairman in World Financial Group. This places him among the top
leaders in the company. His income is high and his team is large
despite the devastation in Puerto Rico caused by Hurricane Ma-
ria in September 2017. Julio relocated to Tampa, Florida, after
the island's power grid was destroyed and when food and basic
resources became scarce. He's now in the process of rebuilding
his team. When I interviewed him in April 2018, his attitude was
sharp, and his spirits were high—pretty impressive considering
it had been only months since his homeland had been effectively
wiped out. I asked him why he chose WFG:

"I wasn't looking for WFG. I knew they existed, and I heard they
were crooks. I was 19, and I believed all of those stories."

The stories to which he's referring are often told on the Internet,
possibly by competitors, and my research proved all of them to
be false.

Julio sees himself as a builder, of both the business and people. I
asked him if that's what it takes to succeed in WFG:

"Not everyone is a builder. It takes years to learn how to become
a builder. People need to learn how to sell so they can make 40 to
50k a year with their own pen while they're learning to become a
builder."

He continued:

"I come from the concept that I don't recruit to become successful; I become successful so I can recruit. I want to attract people. I don't recruit to become a huge success; I become a huge success on my own."

A sales-centric approach to WFG, I thought to myself. Interesting. Most of the people I interviewed seemed to focus more on recruiting, yet Julio suggested becoming successful in selling as a precursor.

I asked him to address the critics who say WFG is a scam, pyramid scheme and cult:

"It's ignorance, and it's a nonprofessional viewpoint. When someone says it's a scam, as a recruiter, you have to question if you really want to work with him or her. When they call WFG a pyramid, I ask them the difference between a pyramid and multilevel marketing. I ask them if they had a bad experience with MLM. If they can describe it, I'll tell them if we are like that. When they claim that it's a cult, I tell them if excitement makes you uncomfortable, this may not be the environment for you. We open our door to everybody, but it's not for everybody."

I made note of his independent aura. All of the leaders seem to possess this. None of them are begging anyone to join, nor are they stalking people at strip malls. These WFG stars know what they have, and it shows in their self-confidence.

I asked Velazquez what he saw as the downside of the opportunity:

"Expectation. You see so many success stories that when someone is new, they create this expectation that it's going to happen overnight. They have to understand that there's a time frame to success. If you don't understand that from day one and keep it real, that it's a process that's going to take five to ten years to become a huge success, the expectation you bring is going to be your downfall."

Brilliant answer. I thought about all the people I've mentored in the writing and speaking business and how they fall into the same trap.

I asked Julio what his greatest joy was in the business:

"When I see people reach their goals and dreams, and not just about money. I love it when they call and say, 'Julio, do you know where I am? I'm at my kid's football game. I couldn't do this when I had a regular job.'"

To wrap up the interview, I asked Velazquez what advice he would offer someone considering WFG as a career:

"Sit down and figure out your goals and dreams. If your goals and dreams can be reached where you're at, you have no business looking at us. But if you can't achieve them with what you're doing, ask yourself if you think you have what it takes to do this. Look at yourself in the mirror and realize that this is all on you, not on your upline or downline. Write down why you're joining this company. If you decide that it's right for you, create a convincing argument and present it to your spouse. You have to convince yourself first, and then convince the person who is going to support you."

He continued:

"Follow your instincts. If your instincts tell you to go for it, then go for it. Give yourself a chance. What have you got to lose? Nothing bad can come out of it."

And that concluded the interview. On a personal note, I found Julio to be highly intelligent, forthcoming and fiercely passionate. I sensed that growing up on a small island and being raised by hardworking parents had made him mentally tough. He appeared to be unfazed by the recent tragedy that had befallen his beloved island. As difficult and challenging as I'm sure it was, his toughness led him to persevere and rebuild in Tampa.

To see the full video interview with Julio Velazquez, visit www.WFGSTARS.com.

CONCLUSION

Even after all these years behind the scenes with World Financial Group, I honestly didn't know what I was going to find when I wrote this book. Anytime you put a microscope over an organization of 70,000 people, there's no telling what you're going to uncover.

This six-month immersion into the inner workings of this opportunity and its leaders hasn't left me in the middle of the proverbial road. I've shared some of these thoughts throughout the chapters. I didn't plan it that way, but every field leader I interviewed, especially the ones we captured on video in our studio at Bona Allen Mansion, inspired me with a surge of emotion that spilled over into the next day's writing. I apologize if this came across too strongly because my goal was to remain objective to allow you to draw your own conclusions. In this way, I may have failed you, dear reader. I didn't expect to get swept up in an emotional tidal wave. I always liked and respected these people, but as I learned their stories, listened to their dreams and experienced their earnestness, I became enamored. I shouldn't have. An author's role in an unauthorized work is to remain neutral and unbiased. I didn't set out to fail, but to my dismay, I'm afraid the evidence is overwhelming.

It required some introspection, but I finally figured out why I fell so hard for the WFG people. Their values are my values. Their dreams are my dreams. Their vision is my vision. I was interviewing myself. A Chinese me. An Indian me. A female and Vietnamese me. I saw myself in each one of them, from the beast-like behavior of Eric Olson to the patriarchal musings of Rich Thawley.

I hope you saw yourself too.

So considering that I started out as an objective insider and eventually crossed over into superfan stalker territory, you'll have to factor in a certain level of pro-WFG bias as you contemplate this content.

If this book got you excited, good for you. If you connected with these people and felt a surge of hope, you may have found a new home. There's no guarantee, but it's possible that you've discovered a business you can build a life around.

And if none of these things happened for you, maybe there's something else out there for which you are better suited. Remember: don't marry the one you like; marry the one you love. Life is too short to settle.

The same principle applies to selecting a business. Select the one that makes you feel that without it, your life wouldn't be as fulfilled.

That's how you stay married for a lifetime. It's also how you have the mental toughness to succeed in business. You fight the good fight because you love it. The people who work only for money never experience the same passion. Quitting never occurs to these people because their love of the business is based not only on money but also on the experience of doing it. I've studied the self- made rich for nearly 35 years, and that's their greatest secret.

I don't know if you will love WFG or not. You won't know unless you try. The question is whether or not you think it's worth a shot.

WFG is neither a perfect company nor a perfect opportunity. Nor are any of the other companies for which I've worked. The difference is that WFG wants to be perfect, and its people want to be better. It's not just a slogan they slap on a wall. They want to be the best and help you do the same. They're earnest in their offer to help you become financially independent, and they sincerely want you to win. Sadly, I don't see that in traditional, cold-hearted corporations. Most are more interested in pleasing stockholders than in the people who make it possible.

World Financial Group is a different kind of company searching for a different kind of person. If you think you're one of those people, then your new business family is waiting for you. Maybe it's time to come home.

RESOURCES

Secrets Self-Made Millionaires Teach Their Kids Workbook
www.secretsworkbook.com

How Rich People Think
www.howrichpeoplethinkbook.com

177 Mental Toughness Secrets of the World Class
www.mentaltoughnesssecrets.com

Mental Toughness University
www.mentaltoughnessuniversity.com

Siebold Success Network Online Store
www.sieboldnetwork.com

Bill Gove Speech Workshop
www.speechworkshop.com

Steve Siebold Media Appearances
www.SteveOnTV.com

Get Tough Retire Rich
www.GetToughRetireRich.com

Expect to Win by Monte Holm
www.MonteHolm.com

Do You Have What It Takes To Ascend To The Throne Of The World-Class?

Can a person of average intelligence and modest means ascend to the throne of the world class? 177 Mental Toughness Secrets of the World Class, identifies and explains the thought processes, habits, and philosophies of the world's greatest performers... and gives you action steps so you can implement these secrets immediately and get what you want.

People Who Adopt These 177 Mental Toughness Secrets Will Be Propelled To The Top... Both Personally and Professionally.

Here's What The World-Class is Saying About This Book:

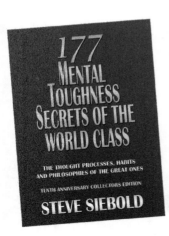

"I find this book and Steve Siebold's mental toughness process to be life changing and liberating. I had a great personal and professional life before I was introduced to mental toughness. After three years of consecutive training, I have a superior life. Steve Siebold is the master of helping people prepare to win."
– Lou Wood
Region Business Director
Johnson & Johnson/OMP

"If you're interested in jump-starting a journey of personal transformation, pick this book up and dive in anywhere. It's a treasure chest of compelling messages and practical exercises. It's up to you to do the work, but Steve Siebold will point you to all the right launching points."
– Amy Edmondson, Ph.D.
Professor of Business
Administration
Harvard Business School

Secrets Self-Made Millionaires Teach Their Kids

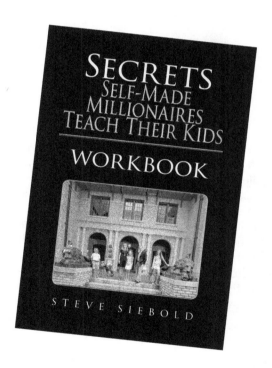

To download FREE workbook please visit:

www.secretsworkbook.com

Do You Think
Like a Millionaire?

This book will teach you how. It compares the thoughts, habits and philosophies of the middle class to the world class when it comes to wealth. The differences are as extreme as they are numerous. The strategy is simple: learn how rich people think, copy them, take action and get rich This book will teach you how. It compares the thoughts, habits and philosophies of the middle class to the world class when it comes to wealth. The strategy is simple: learn how rich people think, copy them, take action and get rich. If you've ever dreamed of living a life most people only see in movies, study this book like a scientist. Freedom from financial worries and a millionaire's lifestyle is closer than you think.

Siebold Success Network is an international network of companies helping individuals and organizations become more successful through professional skills and personal growth training.

visit online store:

www.SieboldNetwork.com

MENTAL TOUGHNESS UNIVERSITY

PSYCHOLOGICAL PERFORMANCE TRAINING

INCREASE SALES AND MOVE MARKET SHARE
BY CREATING A NO EXCUSES-HIGH PERFORMANCE CULTURE

HOME   ABOUT MTU   TESTIMONIALS   FAQ's   CONTACT   MENTAL TOUGHNESS MINUTES

Mental Toughness University is a comprehensive psychological training process
that helps companies increase sales, develop people, and manage change

MENTALTOUGHNESSU.COM

SUBSCRIBE TO THE BLOG

www.mentaltoughnessblog.com

ABOUT THE AUTHOR

Steve Siebold is an internationally recognized authority in the field of psychological performance training. His clients include Johnson & Johnson, Procter & Gamble, Toyota, GlaxoSmithKline, Caterpillar, and hundreds of others.

Since 1984, Siebold has interviewed over 1,300 self-made millionaires and billionaires. His books—177 Mental Toughness Secrets of the World Class, How Rich People Think, Secrets Self-Made Millionaires Teach Their Kids and Get Tough Retire Rich—have been translated into six languages and have sold over 1.2 million copies worldwide.

Siebold has been featured on The Today Show, Good Morning America, CNN World News, the Fox Business Network, CBS News and hundreds of other programs around the world.

Siebold is the past chairman the National Speakers Association's Million Dollar Speakers Club and ranks among the top 1% of professional speakers in the world.

Steve Siebold has been married to Dawn Andrews for 32 years. The couple resides at the historic Bona Allen Mansion near Atlanta.

9 780996 516945